700.92
T

063806

This song remembers

| DATE | | | |
|---|---|---|---|
| | | | |
| | | | |
| | | | |
| | | | |
| | | | |
| | | | |
| | | | |
| | | | |
| | | | |
| | | | |
| | | | |
| | | | |
| | | | |
| | | | |

# This Song Remembers

# This Song Remembers

Self-Portraits of Native
Americans in the Arts

Edited by Jane B. Katz

Houghton Mifflin Company   Boston   1980

**Library of Congress Cataloging in Publication Data**
Main entry under title:

This song remembers.

    1. Indians of North America—Arts—Biography.
I. Katz, Jane B.
E98.A73T45      700′.92′2 [B]      80-20593
ISBN 0-395-29522-X

Printed in the United States of America
10 9 8 7 6 5 4 3 2 1

Copyright acknowledgments on page 203.

To all the creative artists — Indian, Eskimo, and
Aleut — whose spirit songs and migrations of the mind
are here recorded.

# Contents

*Say this: say in my mind*
*I saw your spiders weaving threads*
*to bandage up the day. And more,*
*those webs were filled with words*
*that tumbled meaning into wind.*

*James Welch, Blackfeet*

# Foreword

Upon looking through the manuscript for this book, the first thought that came to me was how marvelous it would be if such a book had been collected a hundred years ago, two hundred years ago, or even further into the past. Such a book would differ from this one, of course, yet the visual arts would be remarkably similar, the music and dance would be only a bit less complex, the literature although recorded from spoken words would be enriched with creative images of the natural world as are the written words that can be found in this book. The great difference, the most important difference, would be that such a book would open to us for the first time the hearts and minds of the natives of America when the invaders came to their land.

Anyone who has attempted to search into the past of America is aware of the one-sidedness of our history. Almost all the written and pictorial records are from the viewpoints of those who came here, not those who lived here. What we know of Native Americans of the past was set down by the intruders upon their land, and the intruders were rarely objective or discerning in their observations. More often than not they regarded the "Indians" as savages, and little effort was made to understand the unique cultures of the various tribes through their ceremonial and visual arts. When the original inhabitants of America were driven from their homes through removals or by wars, their first losses were tangible objects of art, scattered or destroyed by insensitive conquerors. And then in the dark early years of reservation life, they lost a large part of their ceremonial arts.

It is reassuring then to see in this book a renaissance of Native arts. They come forth with freshness at a time when a dreariness haunts the American spirit and a drab sameness seems to overspread the land.

As Jamake Highwater says within: "The twentieth century is rediscovering what it is to be a primal person, to be human. It has finally become apparent that Indians have something to contribute, that we're one of the last reservoirs on earth for this aesthetic mentality — not through our isolation, but through our tenaciousness. We have something urgent to say and something vital to be."

I am glad that I live in the same time as the writers and painters and poets and dancers and singers and other artists who made this book possible. I am grateful to them for letting the world share the feelings of their hearts.

— Dee Brown

# Introduction

Art is a fundamental activity in tribal cultures, an integral part of the daily life of ordinary people. It is an expression of the basic need of people in all times and environments to communicate with others, to record experience and impressions, to cope with a finite existence by passing on something of oneself and one's heritage to future generations.

American Indian and Eskimo cultures, as distinct from Western society, foster the child's innate creativity. In communities and in families that have preserved their tribal heritage, young people learn a wide variety of art forms at home. The Pueblo child makes pots and jewelry; the Navajo learns weaving, basketry, and silversmithing; woodcarving is the hallmark of the Northwest tribes; Eskimos carve in ivory, bone, and stone; beadwork, drawing, and painting are almost universal.

The "art object" is valued not only for aesthetic reasons, as it is in Western society, but also for its utilitarian and religious functions. A Navajo basket is used in healing ceremonies. A Pueblo pot is treasured because the clay comes from Mother Earth and contains "the spirit of those who have gone before."

Creativity is viewed by some tribal people as a gift from the spirits, derived through mystical experience. In tribal ceremonies, aesthetic and spiritual elements blend. Wearing elaborate costumes, Indians and Eskimos sing and dance, paying homage to sacred beings either symbolically or because they accept the reality of the spirit world. The line between real and unreal, between past and present, fades when out of legend steps the yei or kachina of the Southwest tribes, a masked figure impersonating the deity, and dances to the beat of a drum. It is the people's way of communing with cosmic forces, insuring the growth of crops, the perpetuation of all life, and their continued harmony with earth and sky.

In tribal society, the oral language is the primary form of communication, an educational tool as well as a survival mechanism. Through song and story, the child learns the tribe's origin myths and the significance of those entities that exist on a spiritual as well as a physical plane: Mother Earth, Father Sky, the sacred Blue Lake, the Encircling Mountains. Stories relate the interaction of humans with spirits from the woods and from the worlds beyond. Dramatized legends chronicle the adventures of culture heroes, keeping them alive. The past "is a visual memory of dreams and stories retold in the present."[1] The mystical and mythical world of the unseen becomes tangible, for it is expressed in concrete terms.

A variety of art forms — music, song, narration, mime, dance, as well as the plastic and graphic arts — are integrated in tribal ceremonies. People from all walks of life participate in the festivals, creating costumes, masks, and scenic effects, and singing, dancing, and drumming, and the result is a genuine community "happening." Many of the ceremonies follow patterns established hundreds of years ago and thus link the people with centuries of tradition.

From this heritage tribal people draw inspiration, and the arts flourish. The Pueblo poet Simon Ortiz writes of his father's sensitivity to words, sights, and sounds, and of spiritual strength derived from other Acoma elders. "I humbly acknowledge the source" of my creativity, he writes. At the same time, the artist is an individual, an innovator, caught up in the currents of twentieth-century techniques and trends, influenced by them, influencing them in turn, breathing new life into essentially old forms, moving in new directions. Sculptor Allan Houser says: "Nothing will hold me back. I'm reaching for the stars."

One responds intuitively to the vibrant color and diverse patterns of Native American art, to poetry, music, and dance. But when the art forms are viewed against the backdrop of tribal culture, it is possible to attain new levels of perception. Then one becomes aware of the impact of tribal traditions, lore, and symbolism on the artist, and of the evolutionary process each art form has undergone. This cultural and historical frame of reference is what the Native American artist provides when he or she talks about the inspiration for a painting, a song, a theatrical work.

The nineteenth-century wars are over, but Native Americans, the descendants of the dispossessed, have had to face new assaults in the twentieth century: the appropriation of their land and dwindling natural resources and attempts to obliterate their language and culture and deprive them of autonomy. There is the paradox of life in America today — widening opportunities for the educated and talented, but increasing alienation for those who do not "make it" in the dominant culture. In the face of mounting pressures from a materialistic society that claims to be, but has not proved itself, morally superior, some tribal people choose not to get caught up in the "success syndrome." They cling to the old ethic of sharing, dedication to the community, and living on intimate terms with the universe.

Native Americans are creating sculpture, paintings, poems, plays, books, films, and symphonies that reflect pride in their ethnic identity. But they are not afraid to confront the complexities of life today experienced by those of their people still scarred by white society's attempts at cultural genocide, those who live in a twilight world, unsure of who they are. "I sing the songs of both our summer and our winter," writes singer Buffy Sainte-Marie.

The Native American artist is reaching out to the public, trying to create an improved climate for Native people. But there is some ambivalence about that public role, the fear that "success" in white society's terms may mean a negation of traditional tribal values and separation from one's own people. Always, the people come first.  To lose sight of that is a betrayal.  It is with such fundamental issues that the Native American creative artist must come to terms.

On what basis were individuals selected for this book?  The choice was purely subjective.  Artists were chosen because of their distinct contribution in a particular field and for their ability to articulate influences and aspirations.  It seemed valid to have a variety of art forms, regions, and tribes represented, but no attempt was made to be all-inclusive.  Most important, I sought out artistic people who have been close to the source of tribal traditions.  For contrast, I also interviewed people who have departed from those traditions, forging new paths in art.

My previous work with Native Americans taught me the importance of shedding preconceived notions.  The refusal of many Indian people to become what white society wants them to be is their strength.  I approached them as a learner, with great respect for their knowledge, and they shared their lives with me.  With a tape recorder, I traveled to various parts of this country and to Canada, conducting in-depth interviews focusing on an individual's early life, artistic development, and personal philosophy, and the passing along of a tribe's values and traditions.  Because of the book's humanistic focus, I felt it was important to explore some contemporary issues that affect Native Americans and, in fact, all human beings.  I rearranged the material and edited when necessary to insure clarity and logical flow of ideas, but sought to preserve the spontaneity of the taped conversations.  The edited versions were submitted to each of the interviewees for their corrections and approval.  Material obtained from sources other than personal interviews was included in the book to demonstrate the link between oral and written communication in Native American society.

This book is not a survey of Indian and Eskimo arts and artists.  It is by no means intended to be comprehensive.  Nor is it an objective analysis of art forms.  That I leave to others, experts in their fields: Dorothy Dunn, Frederick Dockstader, Clara Lee Tanner, Norman Feder, Bill Holm, Guy and Doris Montham, Dorothy Jean Ray, and others in the visual arts; Margot Astrov,

Herbert Joseph Spinden, Frank Waters, Ruth Underhill, and Jerome Rothenberg in literature and ceremony. This is only a partial list of those to whose work I turned for information and perspective as this book took shape.

Oral history is part of the time-honored tradition of Native Americans, who are accustomed to looking backward: They cannot afford to forget their past. At the same time, they often seem to be able to view the present with clarity, the future with vision. They touch our lives, challenging us to re-examine our premises.

*This Song Remembers* is a medley of personal experiences and perceptions that document a people's migration from yesterday to today. "I have had an unusual life," says the Eskimo artist Pitseolak, "being born in a skin tent and living to hear that two men have landed on the moon."

The individuals whose life histories are presented here are, in my view, uniquely gifted. Their work provides tangible evidence of the vitality and viability of Native American art forms, both traditional and contemporary. Drawing strength from the past, they move forward into the future.

> *It's a duty with me,*
> *I know, to find the horizons* . . .

writes the poet Simon Ortiz. Their art is an extension of their lives, an expression of enduring values. They affirm the inviolability of the tribal consciousness, of the human spirit, and of the earth.

# Part 1
# The Visual Arts

*I paint my impression of Navajo spiritual
beings. It's a way of getting closer to the
unseen . . . I relive my dreams in my paintings.
I can visit many places in my dreams.*

*Mary Morez*

# 1  Arts of the Far North

*When I was young,*
*every day was as a beginning*
*of some new thing.*
        *Eskimo song*

Calling themselves Inuit, "the human ones," Eskimos sing of life. They paint the enchanted world of sea animal and land spirit, aglow with colors rarely present in their stark environment.

Since time immemorial, from materials found on their terrain, Eskimos have made objects both beautiful and utilitarian — an engraved ivory pipe, a ceremonial mask, a bear hewn from white stone. They do not have a word for "art" or "artist." They do have a cultural heritage that places a value on creativity for personal satisfaction and a belief that "one must do a thing properly."

Most of Eskimo art developed after the arrival of Europeans. In the nineteenth century, walrus tusks, bows, and knife handles of ivory were incised with designs of village life. Today, the scope of Arctic and Alaskan arts is extraordinary, encompassing wood and stone cuts, engravings, and lithographs; etchings; paintings in oil, water color, and acrylics; drawing with pencil and felt-tip pen; skin, hide, and yarn appliqué, and sculpture and carving. Eskimos have responded to the influx of new ideas, techniques, and materials brought in by outsiders, but the sensitivity, perceptiveness, and innovation they bring to their work are indigenous.

Along the barren coast of Cape Dorset in Canada's Northwest Territories live a few hundred Inuit who are hunters, carvers, needleworkers, singers, and dancers, people who care for their families and for each other. Not far away is the Eskimo village of

Baker Lake.  Until the 1950s, residents of both settlements lived in isolated camps, subject to harsh extremes of weather, their subsistence and a barter economy dependent on the unpredictable migrations of the caribou.  With the attrition of the caribou came starvation and death.  In 1957, the Canadian government established civil administration over these areas, set up homes and schools for the people, and under the auspices of the Canadian Handicrafts Guild, encouraged the production of arts and crafts. James Houston, a Canadian artist, was instrumental in the founding of the first Eskimo-owned and -operated cooperative for the production and distribution of native artwork.  Houston taught the Cape Dorset Inuit to incise designs on soft green soapstone as they had, for generations, on bone and ivory.  After experimentation, they learned to transfer their designs from the inked stone to light Japanese paper, using a small handpress in a process similar to the Japanese woodcut.  There was increased activity in carving and sculpture, a revival of the ancient women's art of skin appliqué — the sewing of designs cut from hides onto clothing and other useful objects — and the introduction of new · crafts such as batik, macramé, and silk-screening.

Mrs. Alma Houston played an important role in developing sales, marketing techniques, and exhibits worldwide.  Cape Dorset, Baker Lake, and other native villages developed into thriving artists' colonies, with sales of artwork providing a stable income and improved housing and quality of life for the Eskimo.  One of Cape Dorset's most prolific printmakers is Kenojuak, whose plumed birds, animals, and spirits of sun and moon have won her international recognition.  Baker Lake graphic artist Jessie Oonark is noted for intricately patterned prints and for tapestries displaying her superb sense of design, symmetry, and balance.

The contemporary Alaskan Eskimo artist is just as likely to be college-educated and from an urban center as from a remote village.  Art institutes and government-sponsored arts programs have brought young Alaskan Eskimos into contact with new media and techniques, and with international modern art trends, which are reflected in their work.  Among the most influential of the native

Bernard Katexac, *Seasons of the Arctic, III*. Color woodcut, 1977. Courtesy Anchorage Historical and Fine Arts Museum.

Alaskan artists is Joseph Senungetuk of Wales, who has won acclaim for his abstract and expressionistic prints and woodcarvings. Bernard Katexac has produced remarkable woodcuts, etchings, and engravings that record the old way of life in a dramatic, individualistic style. Of his work he says:

> I did many prints using soapstone and woodblocks. Then for two years I suffered a paralyzing attack on the right side of my body. But I was able to complete *Sea-*

*sons of the Arctic,* which was commissioned by the state.

Mostly these days I'm etching on walrus tusks, using my homemade Japanese knife. This process is quicker than carving the woodblocks and brings a higher price.

I used to carve medicine man masks out of laminated red wood. They were six feet high, and were painted red. The upper lip and forehead were painted white with paint used for model airplanes. I used to carve Walrus Masks, and wore them when I danced. Now I can't dance much.[2]

For the Eskimo sculptor or carver, all art has a purpose, either ornamental or cabalistic. The hunter carves an animal to evoke it, or to propitiate its spirit after the killing. The carving is

an act, not an object, a ritual, not a possession . . . The image of the animal whose meat is sought or whose aid has been secured through a dream is thought to be equivalent to the creature itself; carving its image brings

Karlik, *Bird.* Courtesy Minister of Supply and Services, Canada. Reprinted from *Innunnit: The Art of the Canadian Eskimo,* by W. T. Larmour.

it within the influence of the hunter's spirit . . . The carver examines a piece of ivory to find its hidden form. He carves aimlessly until he sees it, humming or chanting as he works. The form emerges. It was always there; he didn't create it; he released it . . .[3]

Traditionally it was the Eskimo men who carved, but in recent years, women have mastered the art. Ida Eyetoak, a Baker Lake carver, says that she studies the stone for inspiration. "I just follow the rock. At first it was quite difficult, but now I almost know as soon as I see the stone what the carving will be."[4]

Ayii-Ayii,
*I think over again my small adventures*
*When with the wind I drifted in my kayak*
*And thought I was in danger.*
*My fears,*
*Those small ones that seemed so big,*
*For all the vital things*
*I had to get and to reach.*
*And yet there is only one great thing,*
*The only thing,*
*To live to see the great day that dawns*
*And the light that fills the world.*[5]

     *Eskimo kayak song*

# Pitseolak,
# Eskimo graphic artist

*In the hazy, treeless world of the Eskimo in Canada's eastern Arctic not so long ago, spirits danced, casting stark shadows against the snows. Shamans chanted musical incantations to spirits and to animals, both loved and feared.*

*In such a world around the turn of the century, in Hudson Bay in the Northwest Territories, Pitseolak was born, the child of migrants. Her father followed the caribou across the icy tundra. When her family settled on Cape Dorset, her mother cooked, prepared skins, sewed clothing, and kept the oil fires burning. Like the mythical young Eskimo girl Sedna who escaped from her husband, a cruel bird, and returned to her parents only to be abandoned by them, a woman was often expendable. This was a male-oriented society.*

*Pitseolak was fortunate. She married Ashoona, a skillful hunter, and they prospered. Though eleven of her seventeen children died, victims of epidemics in the migrant camps, her fatalistic outlook sustained her. As her people moved from an aboriginal existence to modern homes with indoor plumbing, with the snowmobile replacing the dog sled, she adapted.*

*Pitseolak's family is artistic, and all her children are talented carvers and printmakers. Art is their way of life — an art that is elemental and vital, a visual language readily understood by old and young. Like all Eskimo artists, Pitseolak has a long memory.*

*She told her life story to Dorothy Eber, with the aid of Eskimo interpreters, in 1970.*

*In her stone cuts, engravings, and drawings with felt-tip pen, Pitseolak evokes images from past and present, powerful human and animal forms moving in rhythm with the flight of birds, the lumbering of the polar bear. Her colorful figures inhabit their own space, create their own world, forcing us to see, as she sees, beauty in commonplace, everyday experience.*

My name is Pitseolak, the Eskimo word for the sea pigeon. When I see pitseolaks over the sea, I say, "There go those lovely birds — that's me, flying!"

I have lost the time when I was born, but I am old now — my sons say maybe I am seventy . . . I became an artist to earn money, but I think I am a real artist . . . I draw the things I have never seen, the monsters and spirits, and I draw the old ways, the things we did long ago before there were many white men . . .

I had a happy childhood. I was always healthy and never sick. I had a large family — three brothers and a sister — and we were always happy to be together. We lived in the old Eskimo way. We would pick up and go to different camps — we were free to move anywhere and we lived in many camps . . . it depended whether a person wanted to go far or to be near a settlement. My father hunted in the old way, too — with a bow and arrow. He had a shotgun but he didn't use it. Sometimes there were bad winters and we would go hungry, but there was no starvation . . .

Ashoona and I used to be little children together. I don't remember how old I was when I married, but girls got married very young then; now they are older. Ashoona's father took my mother and me on the dog team to Ikirasaq, which is near Sakbuk, a one-day trip from Cape Dorset . . . Because Ashoona was an inland hunter, at our wedding I had on caribou skin clothes . . . Many

women used to be jealous of me because I had such lovely clothes.

When Namoonie, my first son, was born, three women held me. It was like that in the old times — there were always women who helped. Afterward, they would make magic wishes for the child — that a boy should be a good hunter, that a girl would have long hair, and that the child should do well at whatever he was doing. I don't know if it is easier to have babies in a hospital. Ahalona! At any time it is hard. There is a saying, "It is hard but it is well." I had seventeen children — every year I had a baby — and many of them died as little children . . .

Sometimes in the winter it was boring in the igloo, but we never stayed inside much. We had warmer clothes in those days, and it used to be fun when it was windy. The fathers would make toy sleds for their sons and daughters to slide on, and when the children had their sleds and their toy whips, they would play outside most of the day. Now they are in school all day and they have the habit of staying indoors. Very often in those days when we felt happy in camp, Ashoona and I would play the accordion. The little children would come and dance.

My husband died . . . of a very bad sickness. Many people died at that time in the camps and in Cape Dorset. There was no doctor then, and nobody knew what the sickness was. For a long time after Ashoona died we were very sad. Sometimes I thought I would lose my mind. Whenever a dog team came to the camp, Ottochie would go and look for his father. He thought he would find him . . . After Ashoona died we were very poor — and often we were hungry. We were poor until Sowmik [the Eskimos' name for Jim Houston] and the government houses came . . . I think Sowmik was the first man to help the Eskimos. Ever since he came, the Eskimo people have been able to find work. Here in Cape Dorset they call him "The Man" . . .

Jim Houston told me to draw the old ways, and I've been drawing the old ways and the monsters ever since. We heard that Sowmik told the people to draw anything, in any shape, and to put a

At left, Pitseolak at Cape Dorset. Photo: Tessa Macintosh.

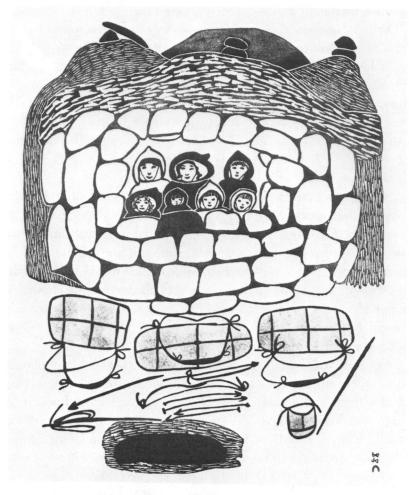

Pitseolak, *Family Camping in Tuniq Ruins.* © 1976 The West Baffin Eskimo Co-operative.

head and a face on it.  He told the people that this drawing was very good . . .  Since the Co-op began, I have earned a lot of money with my drawing.  I get clothes from the drawings, and I earn a living from paper . . .  Does it take much planning to draw?  Ahalona!  It takes much thinking, and I think it is hard to think.  It is hard like housework.

The other day I drew an Eskimo woman with a blue fish spear.

I did not want to leave the fish spear alone; that is why I put the bird on her head. There's a baby hidden inside the parka, too — you can tell by the shape of the parka!

I have had an unusual life, being born in a skin tent and living to hear on the radio that two men have landed on the moon. I think the new times started for Eskimos after the white people's war, when the white men began to make many houses in the Arctic . . . In some ways I like living in a warm house, but in the old days, before all these things happened, we were always healthy. I was never sick, not even with all the children I had. In these later years, I have been sick most of the time and I have

Pitseolak, *Tattooed Woman*. Stone cut, 1963. Courtesy Minister of Supply and Services, Canada. Reprinted from *Innunnit: The Art of the Canadian Eskimo*, by W. T. Larmour.

found each year harder to bear.   Now that we all live in one place, we get sick a lot  . . .

I think the new ways would be better than the old, except that nowadays the young people make so much trouble.   A long time ago when I was bringing up my children, they would do what you told them to do.   If you gave them something to eat, they were grateful and happy about it . . .   Now, all that has changed. They don't listen at all.   People get worse when they all live in one place.   The young people are always in trouble.

I have heard that there is someone — not a human being but a spirit — in the moon.   When I heard that the two men had landed on the moon, I wondered what the spirit thought of these two men landing on his land  . . .

After my husband died, I felt very alone and unwanted; making prints is what has made me happiest since he died.   I am going to keep on doing them until they tell me to stop.   If no one tells me to stop, I shall make them as long as I am well.   If I can, I'll make them even after I am dead.[6]

# Kenojuak,
# Eskimo graphic artist

Time was when all the world lay in darkness, and the raven was the only bird. And like the raven, the world was black. Then owl came . . . For the first time, earth and men were able to walk upright, and others too.

Sometimes I am so full of thought I do not want to sleep. Many are the thoughts that rush off like wings of birds out of darkness. What are thoughts? Are they like songs which just come, drift, and are gone again?

Soon a new day will change my whole life, and the sun will bring light to the whole world.

Kenojuak, *Multifeathered Bird*. Stone cut.

## 2 From the Northwest Coast

*You, whose day it is, make it beautiful,*
*Get out your rainbow colors,*
*So it will be beautiful.*

*Nootka song*

Overlooking richly forested islands, quiet bays, and remote inlets approachable only by canoe, tall carved totem poles of the Northwest tribes still stand. Dignified, whitened with age, they preside over deserted villages, monuments to a way of life that has passed.

The totem pole builders of the Pacific Northwest — a coastal region stretching from Southeast Alaska to the mouth of the Columbia River — were fishing and hunting peoples. Spanish seamen and British traders arriving in the area in the late eighteenth century found a hundred thousand Indian people, sustained by the natural resources that the environment provided. In the rivers were waves of migrating salmon, sea otters, sea lions, seals and whales, clams, and other shellfish. In the dense rain forests, wild game was plentiful, as were berries and other vegetable foods, trees for carving and fibrous barks for woven products. The abundance of land and sea freed the people from the daily preoccupation with food gathering, thus enabling them to develop their culture.

Scattered in independent villages, on islands, and along the rugged coastline were six distinct language groups: Tlingit and Haida, Tsimshian and Kwakiutl, Nootka and Salish. Although politically diverse and divided by the rivalries of kinship groups, they shared homogeneous cultural traits. In great gabled houses of timber and split planks, related families lived together during the long winter, a time for extended feasts, ceremonials, and so-cializing. In the spring and summer, they moved into tempo-rary shelters built of boards and mat and traveled in long, narrow dugout canoes hollowed out of red cedar decorated with totemic animals.

Social and ceremonial patterns of the Northwest tribes were based on common religious beliefs and ancient mores. Each tribe was made up of several clans or family groups claiming descent from a common ancestor represented by a totem animal. Repre-sentations of ravens, thunderbirds, and other mythical ancestors were carved and painted on the lofty poles that adorned house-fronts, and on ceremonial objects. (The word *totem* comes from the Algonkian or Algonquian language-group, and means "brother.") The belief in animism was all-pervasive. The sea, rivers, forests, air, and the underworld were believed to be inha-bited by good and evil spirits that emerged in the winter months. Each man had his spirit protectors. The Shaman was a com-municant between humans and this spirit world. Masks represent-ing animals and humans were useful in conjuring up spirits.

There was no division between art and daily life. On a voyage to the Northwest Coast in 1805, Russian Captain Lisiansky wrote in his logbook: "Carving and painting can be considered the most important art or handicraft of the local population. Judging from the number of masks and many other carved and painted objects I have seen, we may conclude that every man is an artist. Here you will not find a single tool or dish that is not decorated; this is especially true of boxes and chests whose lids are covered with shells that resemble teeth."[7]

The artist sought to preserve the legendary history of his ances-tors and their relationship with the supernatural world. Humans were depicted with animal characteristics. Animals were some-times presented naturalistically, but more often symbolically, in stylized forms. Out of red and yellow cedar, spruce, alder, and hemlock, Northwest peoples carved figures on the prows of their canoes, on headdresses and masks, battle helmets, amulets and fet-ish dishes, cooking vessels, chests, doors, and door-posts. On

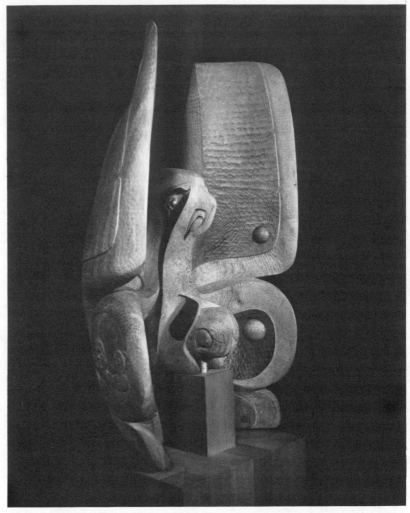

Lawney Reyes, *Eagle Number One*.  Red cedar with bronze inlay, 1976.  Collection of Robert Beaupre.  Photo courtesy of the artist.

hooks used to catch halibut they carved fetish animals, and from the horns of mountain sheep they fashioned festival spoons.

The women wove with great artistry — blankets, robes, hats, and baskets.  Their most notable contribution was the Chilkat robe made by Tsimshian and Tlingit women from the twisted wool of the mountain goat and yellow cedar bark.  The women's designs were not based on mythology or religious beliefs, but were primarily geometric patterns.

Modern technology made inroads in the twentieth century, and the old life inevitably gave way to the new. Many men left the villages to get an education and jobs. The communities were disoriented, their social structures disrupted. As ceremonial and ritual diminished in importance, the arts lost their central place in the people's lives. Still, there were those who continued carving and painting and weaving in the old way, to preserve something from their rich ancestral past.

In the 1960s and 1970s the availability of government funding for ethnic cultural projects made it possible for a new generation to devote itself to revitalizing old art forms. This movement is symbolized by the Daybreak Star Center for the cultural arts in Seattle, Washington, run by Native Americans, decorated with sculpture, carvings, and paintings representing various regions of the United States, a meeting of all tribes through art.

A variety of art styles can be found among Northwest tribes today. Bill Reid, Haida, is widely acclaimed for carvings in wood, silver, and argillite. Other carvers of note are Robert Davidson, Haida; Joe David, Nootka; and Marvin Oliver, Quinault. Lawney Reyes, Colville, produces powerful individualistic sculpture based on Northwest Coast motifs.

# Tony Hunt,
# Kwakiutl woodcarver

*The Kwakiutl, or Kwagulth, a sea-going people, lived on rocky islands separated by deep channels and along the western shores of British Columbia. In an extraordinary record of their life and customs, photographer-historian Edward Curtis wrote in 1915: "The Kwakiutl have no conception of a personified, supreme power. They believe in many spirits — some inhabiting animal bodies, others purely imaginary — which can and do impart supernatural power to men who obtain their pity . . ."*[8] *To acquire protection, the Kwakiutl purified themselves during their winter ceremonials, the most important of which was the potlatch.*

*Tony Hunt is the nephew of Mungo Martin, revered traditional chief and carver of the Kwakiutl, and great-grandson of George Hunt — carver, tribal historian, and interpreter for Edward Curtis. Hunt's work has been featured in major exhibitions, including the Royal Ontario Museum, the Provincial Museum of British Columbia, the Heard Museum in Phoenix, Arizona, and Chicago's Field Museum. He has constructed totem poles on commission by the Mexican government, the cities of Bonn and Buenos Aires, and the University of Victoria in British Columbia. He has taught traditional design and carving techniques at the Provincial Museum, and at 'Ksan, a reconstructed Indian vil-*

*lage dedicated to the preservation of traditional art forms. He has appeared on television and in films, among them* Legend of the Magic Knives *and* The Land Is the Culture.

*Song to Killer Whale*

*Going round the world I was carried on the water by the long-life giver, with your magic supernatural power.*
*Flitting about on the water, poor I, with your long-life giver, with your magic supernatural power.* [9]

I was born on Alert Bay in 1942 and spent my childhood in Fort Rupert, a Kwagulth village on Vancouver Island. My father was a logger and a fisherman, as well as a woodcarver. My mother raised me in the early years. I was sent to public school, but it was my Uncle Mungo Martin — I called him "Grandfather" — who was really responsible for my education.

Mungo Martin was one of the highest-ranking chiefs of our clan, the Walas Kwagulth. Because I was a first-born son and destined to be chief, he chose me to carry on the traditions of our people. He possessed many skills. He was a trapper and built his own boats. He learned how to operate a tape recorder so that he could record, and thus preserve, our tribal songs. He was a woodcarver and worked for the Provincial Museum in British Columbia. He built the longhouse that is on display there in the style of his family's ancestral home.

I followed Mungo Martin everywhere. He taught me the origin and significance of our family's crests, our songs and legends. When we were out walking, he'd suddenly sit down and sing an old song that he'd just recalled, repeating the words many times. Again and again, he told me the story of Raven, an all-white bird who lived in a longhouse. Ignoring warnings, Raven opened a forbidden box, and out came the sun and the moon. They flew

Tony Hunt. Photo courtesy of Images for a Canadian Heritage.

out of the longhouse through the smokehole.  Panicking, Raven
followed them out through the smokehole, and he turned black.

   My apprenticeship as an artist with Mungo Martin lasted ten
years.  He taught me the long-established rules of Northwest Coast
carving and painting.  Whatever medium the artist uses, the design principles are the same.  For example, a formline usually sur-
rounds a design, inside of which the design seems to float.  Our
artists are not restricted in colors, as are other Northwest Coast
tribes, but tradition determines where the colors will be placed.
Mungo introduced me to the motifs of Kwagulth art — certain
animal, fish, and bird forms that recur, suggesting our kinship
with these creatures.  I learned to carve the Sisutl, the double-
headed snake with one body that appears on our drums and belts

and on huge flat boards that are displayed at our winter ceremonials. Similar serpent images have been found on remnants of Chinese art dating back to the sixth century and in the art of ancient India. I learned to carve animal headdresses made of wood and decorated with felt, abalone shells, and paint.

The most challenging task I undertook was the construction of transformation masks, which are technically very difficult to execute. The raven mask relates to stories of raven transforming himself into a human being. With one pull of a string, the mask opens, and a moon's face with human characteristics appears. Pull the string again, and the raven reappears. It suggests the raven's supernatural powers, and it is very theatrical.

Mungo conveyed to me his respect and feeling for his work. An artist must not work for money alone. He may make a living selling art to tourists. His work may be displayed in a major museum. But he must never stop learning. He must continually strive to win recognition from his elders. The real measure of an artist's success comes when he's asked to carve a mask for a sacred ceremony. In my ten years of apprenticeship with Mungo Martin, I absorbed a hundred years of tradition.

Without any outside support, I set up a workshop that evolved into a gallery for the display and marketing of Indian-made work, and over the years I've taught many people who have become accomplished carvers. A ten-year training period is essential, during which one learns all the rules and traditions. Then one can begin to bend the rules a little. But if one bends them too much, he will not be respected. Some contemporary carvers do not have this background. They don't know their tribal language, and they don't know how the art objects are used in the ceremonies. I find their work empty.

In my role as teacher, I pass on my knowledge of the connection between our art and our religion. Unlike other Northwest Coast tribes, the Kwagulth never submitted entirely to Christianity. Even after the potlatches were outlawed by the government because the missionaries said they were pagan, we continued to hold them in secret. They were held to commemorate a birth or death, to initiate a new home, and to validate the rights and privileges of a chief.  When Mungo Martin built the longhouse at the Provincial Museum in 1955, he said that without a potlatch it wouldn't be a real longhouse, and the government gave us permission to hold one.  I took part in the dancing; I did the Bee Dance, which I've done since I was a boy.  Since that time, potlatching has been permitted.

In recent years, I've begun to assume my leadership role within the tribe.  I must sit with the chiefs to learn the words of the songs that tell of mythological beings and events.  This is difficult, for the songs have been passed down for hundreds of years, and the language has undergone many changes during that time.  I must learn the art of speechmaking, so that I can preside at ceremonial occasions.  Most important, I must learn to perform the dances meticulously, without mistakes.  In the old days, if you made a

Tony Hunt, Hok Hok or bird-monster mask, worn by dancer in potlatch in memory of the artist's mother.  Photo courtesy of the artist.

mistake, they threw you into the fire. I've been dancing since I was five years old. At nineteen, I was initiated into the most important dance society, the Hamatsa, which re-creates the ancient Cannibal Dance symbolically. My goal in dancing, as in carving, is to win the recognition of the elders.

I'm a very down-to-earth person. I'm a businessman. My gallery has made it possible for Indians to market their work successfully. I've traveled to Germany to demonstrate Northwest Coast carving styles and to Japan to take part in the World Craft Council. I drive a 262 C Volvo car. But when I put on a mask and costume and step into the longhouse for a potlatch, I feel that I'm in touch with my ancestors. I pay my respects to the past.[10]

*Kwakiutl Cradle Song*

. . . *When I am a man, then I shall be a harpooner, O father!*
    *Ya ha ha ha.*
*When I am a man, then I shall be a canoebuilder, O father!*
    *Ya ha ha ha.*
*When I am a man, then I shall be an artisan, O father!*
    *Ya ha ha ha . . .*
*That we may not be in want, O father!*
    *Ya ha ha ha.*[11]

# John Hoover,
# Aleut sculptor

*More than eight thousand years ago, Asian peoples drifted across the Bering land bridge and settled the mountainous Aleutian Islands off the coast of Alaska. Ingeniously exploiting the resources of land and sea, they developed a hunting and fishing culture similar to that of the Eskimo, based on cooperation and sharing of provisions. In songs, dances, and other ritual observances they acknowledged a creator. Shamans, both male and female, were empowered to intercede with ancestors and with supernatural forces.*

*Russian occupation and the United States' purchase of Alaska in 1868 disrupted Aleutian village life. Missionaries undermined the influence of the shaman. The gradual depletion of the sea otter and fish led to an exodus from the villages.*

*John Hoover was born in Cordova, a city in Southwest Alaska, in 1919. Although his mother was Aleut, he was brought up with little knowledge of his heritage. Hoover is a commercial fisherman. He is also largely a self-taught artist. His earliest works were seascapes, which he sold to fellow fishermen. An interest in woodcarving led him to explore the themes and techniques of traditional Northwest Coast art, but he longed for an art form that would give his imagination free reign. Thus began a search back into the past for an understanding of the art of his ancestors and the development of a highly personal style influenced by ancient Eskimo and Northwest Coast traditions, particularly shamanism.*

*Hoover's sculpture, which has been exhibited all over the world, captures the beauty and spirit of Northwest Coast marine life. Elongated sculptural shapes seem to rise out of the water. Sea creatures and birds intermingle with human forms in Hoover's world of myth and magic.*

I was born in Cordova, Alaska, and grew up in an urban environment. My father was German. My mother was Aleut. She had been orphaned as a child, and had been adopted by Russian priests. The Russians who colonized the Aleutian Islands desecrated the native population. They forced men and boys to go on dangerous fishing expeditions — from which many never returned — in pursuit of the valuable sea otter. The women, too, were exploited. My mother was virtually enslaved, forced to do menial labor for the Russian clergy. She went from family to family, from village to village. When she came of age, she escaped and developed her own identity, eventually becoming educated, marrying, and settling in Cordova.

My father died when I was seven, and Mother supported the family by fishing, working in canneries, laundries, and mining camps, and as a camp cook in the oil fields. There were many facets to her personality. She loved music and managed to provide lessons for my sisters. One became a concert violinist and was to study in Europe, but leukemia ended her life at the age of eighteen. Although my mother became a cultivated woman, she never forgot how to tan a bird's hide. She used to trim my sisters' clothing with goose- and swan's-down. We spent many enjoyable hours reverting back to our lost culture, finding and eating raw seafoods in the lakes and on ocean beaches.

Because mother had suffered as an Aleut, she wanted us to fit into the mainstream. She dressed us in starched white clothes and sent us to public schools and to the Presbyterian Church. As it turned out, I was accepted by some and rejected by others.

Cordova was an international city and had everything from a symphony to street gangs. While my sister attended orchestra rehearsals, I expressed myself by taking part in gang wars. These weren't really racial conflicts, although there was plenty of animosity toward nonwhites and that increased the tension. As a U.S. territory under federal law, Alaska was administered by federal marshals. They were power moguls who intimidated the natives, invaded their homes, and pillaged their art until there was nothing left of the culture.

I learned to draw by watching my older sister sketch. I thought it was a form of magic, and I imitated her. After high school, I played the drums in a band. I did every kind of job imaginable. I drove a cab, worked in the canneries and on the railroads, and dug clams. I had been fishing since I was nine years old, and salmon fishing became my livelihood.

Fishing is a precarious existence, for the elements are beyond your control. But it can be lucrative. To this day, I return to Alaska every year during the salmon-fishing season. Prices are skyrocketing. I could make a lot of money. But I earn just enough to provide for my family during the year, and then I come home. Let the younger men stay on. They need more money.

I moved to Washington, where I took classes in fine art and began painting in earnest. A friend and I built a large wooden fishing vessel in our backyard, a fifty-eight-foot Alaska limit-seiner. We didn't have enough power tools and had to shape the timbers by hand. They were beautiful shapes — curved, sculpted, abstract — and I became interested in sculpture.

I began by reproducing traditional Northwest carvings — totemic animal and bird figures. But I felt inhibited by the rigid structure of this very formal art and experimented with my own interpretations. I used the traditional colors of Northwest Coast art. For inspiration, I read Northwest Coast myths and legends. I loved stories of people who had relationships with animals. The interrelating of humans with nonhuman beings became a central theme in my work.

I spent some time as a visiting artist in the Orient. I marveled

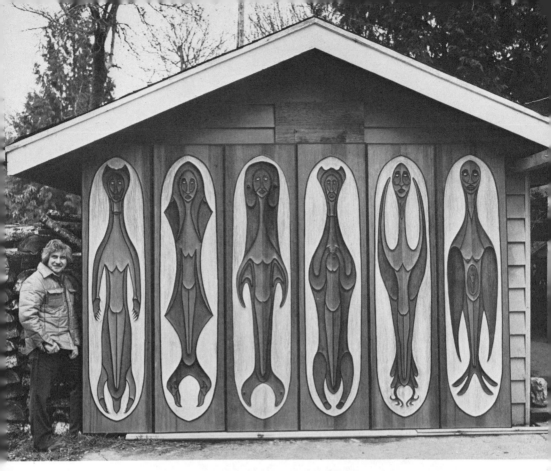

John Hoover with *Ancestor Spirit Boards.* Polychromed carved cedar panels. From left to right: Bear, Salmon, Killer Whale, Wolf, Eagle, Raven. Photo: Mary Randlett © 1975. Artist's collection.

at the Japanese temples — beautiful, elaborate structures made by priests. I found Filipino and Taiwanese woodworkers to be master craftsmen, capable of reproducing an image exactly as they saw it with great precision, and I learned their carving techniques just by watching. I found only one man making ancestor figures, much like those of the ancient Eskimos, and resembling those I was then carving. I felt that I was helping to revive an almost lost art.

From childhood, I had been intrigued by fantasy and the occult, and the spirit world was very real to me. Shamanistic figures began to appear in my work. For the shaman, pieces of wood, rocks, and stones are alive and possess energy. A rock has a body,

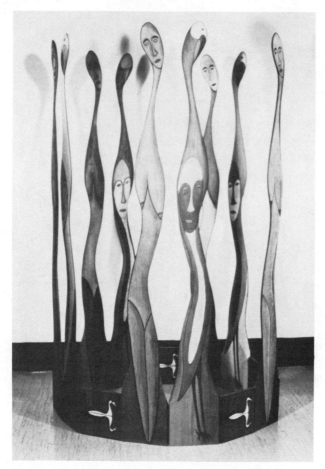

John Hoover, *Winter Loon Dance*. Polychromed carved
cedar. Photo: Guy Montham. Artist's collection.

a log has grain. The shaman or healer delivers commands to the
spirit, using drums, flutes, even manufactured noisemakers to
drive evil forces away. He or she induces trances and brings about
transformation from one form of life to another. There is often
some form of mystical rebirth. Shamans are the original psychol-
ogists. They draw out images from the subconscious. They bring
what is fearful out in the open, so that people can cope with it.
Like the shaman, the tribal artist communicates with the spirit

world, not just through the finished product, but during the creation of it. This communication is a continuous process.

My work isn't threatening. The faces are gentle and peaceful. The images are stylized. To achieve muted color tones and the effect of natural pigments, I mix paints with white diluted with turpentine. I like the soft washes of orange, rust, wood tones, the blue-greens of the sea. The wood that I use is cedar, four or five hundred years old.

Loons have always followed me, like spirit protectors. Once when I was fishing, a loon circled my boat for about twenty minutes, crying and crying, and then disappeared. Later, when I picked up my net, two loons — a male and a female — were entangled in it, side by side. One had been the first to die. The other, unable to save its mate, had joined it in death.

My life is a search for something beyond the ordinary experience. I have sailed from my home on Puget Sound to Alaska in my limit-seiner. I'd like to have a telescope powerful enough to see into other planets. I'd like to try hang-gliding, to soar in the air for hours.

Sometimes I feel as if there's an immense gulf separating me from the spirit world. My creativity is an attempt to cross that gulf. I hope that the spirituality of my work comes through to others. There's more to it than just materials. There has to be some mystery to life. [12]

A *Shaman's Magic Song*

*You earth,*
*Our great earth!*
*See, oh see:*
*All these heaps*
*Of bleached bones*
*And wind-dried skeletons!*
*They crumble in the air,*
*The mighty world,*
*The mighty world's*
*Air!*
*Hey-hey-hey!* [13]

# 3 From the Woodlands

At the time of Columbus' arrival in the New World, approximately two hundred thousand Indians occupied territory extending eastward from the Mississippi River to the Atlantic Coast, and from what is now Tennessee into eastern Canada.

From the northern shores of the Great Lakes to the Canadian Arctic is the homeland of the Canadian Cree and Ojibway peoples. These Indians have developed a distinctive school of painting rooted in their fast-fading oral tradition. Inspiration for the work of the Canadian legend painters comes from paintings found on flat rock surfaces surrounding lakes and from the illustrated birch bark scrolls of the Midewiwin, an ancient religious society whose rituals centered around healing the sick. One of the founders of this art form is Norval Morrisseau, an Ojibway from Ontario, who was the first to break tribal taboos forbidding the presentation of sacred lore in pictorial form for the white man to see. Morrisseau was denounced for "profaning" the legends: ". . . there were rumors that Morrisseau had been 'cursed' by several religious leaders. Morrisseau persisted in his painting activity, however, and demonstrated by his survival (with no apparent ill effects) that it was possible to do this kind of art and survive." [14]

Other first-rate Canadian artists, among them Jackson Beardy, Cree/Saulteaux, and Daphne Odjig, Odawa, join with Morrisseau in creating colorful, imaginative works expressing the unity of man

Daphne Odjig, *In Search of Identity*.   Acrylic, 1979.   Photo courtesy of the artist.

and nature.   Odjig is more than a legend painter.   Her mystical works are highly symbolic, with images of the thunderbird, the drum, Mother Earth, and the powwow recurring.   She identifies with the modernist school of painting, particularly Picasso.

Farther south, Minnesota's lake country is the ancestral home of Chippewa/Ojibway people closely allied with the Canadians in philosophy and traditions.   The abundance of water, wild game, and hardwood forests shaped the lifestyle of these Indians, who had a complex religious system and refined arts.   They constructed wooden bowls, spoons, war clubs, and effigies used in sacred "medicine bundles." Rawhide was used for bags and clothing. The Great Lakes tribes excelled in beadwork and quillwork. Their elaborate floral patterns are still much in evidence today in costume design using colorful ribbon appliqué — the overlapping of wide bands of silk ribbons used to trim women's garments.

The intermingling of the Chippewa with other tribes and ethnic groups in the area led to an exchange of ideas and values that affected their art. The paintings of Chippewa artist Carl Gawboy capture the diversity and spirit of the people of the north woods. "I paint life in the area in the 1920s and 1930s: the loggers at work, Finns hauling wood with horses, an Indian's cabin overlooking a lake, an old woman pushing a canoe, another carrying a child. These people lived in poverty during the depression years, far from stores and hospitals, and suffered great privations. Still, they were ambitious, hard-working and adaptable."

Gawboy is pleased with changes over the last two decades that have enabled Indians to assume greater control of their own lives.

Carl Gawboy, *The Gill-Net*. Watercolor, 1976. Private collection. Photo courtesy of the artist.

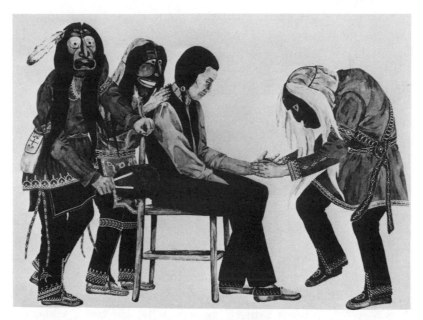

Richard Hill. *Ashes Purification*. (A depiction of the Iroquois "False Face" ceremonial.) Watercolor. Artist's collection.

Improved housing and schooling and government training programs have given Indians access to better jobs, and thus economic stability, on which, he says, their cultural survival depends. "Today there is a renaissance of the old art forms. The powwow circuit has been enriched in the last twenty years. There are intertribal ceremonies, some secret. Now songs and dances are performed. The artists display their work — new designs in garments, beadwork, painting, and carving, many inspired by nineteenth-century motifs. The tribal art forms continue to evolve, and yet there is continuity. They represent the best of the worlds of yesterday and today."[15]

Tribes of the Northeast woodlands were seminomadic, subsisting on hunting, fishing, and some agriculture. Using the abundant wood found in their environment, they carved masks for their sacred False Face ceremonies. Out of hemp and cornhusks they created baskets and other fiber products. Shell beads called wampum were used in the creation of pictographic belts that served as message-conveyers from tribe to tribe and as barter or currency. Their beadwork style consisted of white beads in delicate designs on a dark cloth background. They were skilled silversmiths.

Woodlands culture was in decline for many generations. White men's wars, disease, relocation, and intermarriage led to a dwindling of the Indian population. But the art forms, reflecting thousands of years of tradition, survived. At the center of the resurgence of artistic and ceremonial life of the Northeastern tribes is the new Native American Center for the Living Arts in Niagara Falls, built in the form of a turtle to suggest the symbolic animal on whose back the Iroquois believe the world was created. One of its founders is Duffy Wilson, a Tuscarora Indian who for many years carved images from Iroquois legends in stone. More than 600 Iroquois in New York State, Ontario, and Quebec are today involved in "the living arts," which are closely connected with Iroquois religion. Tuscarora painter Richard Hill comments:

Non-Indians build great temples or cathedrals as places of worship. We believe that the works of the Creator — trees, mountains, lakes, rivers, and other land formations are inherently sacred, and these are our places of worship. We live by spiritual messages. Our ceremonial objects are a living force that has the power to help us. They should not be placed on display on museum shelves, but must be properly cared for by the tribes. [16]

Once an endless sea world of complete darkness flowed beneath a huge dome-shaped sky. Its only inhabitants were sea animals and birds. Above the sky dome, in long bark houses and wearing clothes of deer hides, lived beings that looked like humans . . . One of them, Sky Woman, fell through a hole in the sky. A flock of birds carried her safely down to the water on their interlocked wings. They held a council to decide where to put the woman; the turtle offered his back. Land began to grow there, and a huge island, created in the sea world on the turtle's back became North America. The Iroquois still call this continent "Great Turtle Island." [17]

*Iroquois creation story*

# Peter Jemison,
## Seneca painter

*On scattered reservations in New York State and Canada live the
Six Nations of the Iroquois — Seneca, Mohawk, Oneida, Onon-
daga, Cayuga, and Tuscarora Indians — who call themselves the
Hodenosaunee, "the Longhouse People." They still gather today in
a symbolic longhouse to rededicate themselves to the principles of
law and brotherhood that over the centuries have welded them
together.*

*The Hodenosaunee worship an invisible creative force. Women
play a decisive role in their government. A Council of Chiefs, with
representatives from each of the tribal groups, passes measures af-
fecting all the nations, but only after consensus is reached. This
early form of democracy is believed by some to have set the pattern
for the framing of the United States Constitution.*

*A professional artist dedicated to the preservation of Indian art
and culture, Peter Jemison has re-expressed traditional Iroquois
symbols in a book he illustrated:* The Iroquois and the Founding of
the American Nation. *He has established community programs for
Indians and has directed the Seneca Nation Organization for the
Visual Arts and the American Indian Culture Center in Buffalo,
New York. Currently, Jemison directs the gallery of the American
Indian Community House in New York City, which presents and
promotes the art of Native Americans from North and South
America. He is a member of the New York State Iroquois Confer-*

*ence and an advisor to the New York State Department of Educa-*
*tion, and has developed television programs for Indian children.*

My work and my life are closely bound to Indian people and Indian culture. I grew up on the fringe of the Cattaraugus Reservation in upstate New York. My parents are both Seneca, but they're nontraditional, and I was raised Presbyterian. I had to find my own way as an Indian.

I went to the white man's schools. In high school and college, I adapted to academic life. I was a good student, an athlete, a class officer. I took all sorts of courses, from literature to physics, which at the time seemed to be a hindrance. All I really wanted was to develop as an artist. But as it turned out, this broad education has been extremely valuable to me in finding employment.

After graduation, I studied Italian art and culture at the University of Siena in Italy. I learned to draw by studying the work of the great old Italian masters. I held a variety of jobs — as a display artist, as an art teacher. I worked as a counselor for children with mental and physical disabilities. Gradually, I gravitated back to Indian communities. I learned how to write grant proposals and obtained government funding to set up education and art programs and community outreach programs for Indians on my home reservation.

I had a white man's education, but none of my formal education had given me any understanding of Indian art and culture. And that was true of so many Indians of my generation. I began a period of five years of really intensive training. I resolved to learn all the old art forms directly from the elders. For the various community programs that I was involved in, I hired beadworkers, costume designers, leather-craft workers, silversmiths, and carvers to teach and demonstrate their art. I tried to find older people who had been involved in the tradition — longhouse people, for ex-

Peter Jemison. Courtesy of the artist.

ample. Younger people came to learn the art forms they had heard about but had never really experienced. And I learned with them. Soon, I was making moccasins, carving in steatite (a form of stone), and forming an eagle on the bowl of a pipe, using red pipestone. I learned how to carve False Face masks out of basswood and poplar in the style of the ancients. These masks are sacred objects. As far back as our people can recall, they've been a part of our religion, they have been helping us on earth. They are used today in our curing or medicine ceremonies. Members of the False Face Society enter our homes, extinguish the fire in the stove, blow the ashes onto the people as a form of purification, then play pranks, dance, and depart. It seemed valid to me to perpetuate this old art, a form of iconography.

The elders gave of themselves, transmitted their skills and spiritual values to anyone who would learn. Gradually, the missing links in my education were filled in. I studied all forms of native art, like bone carving. That's an intricate art that goes back hundreds of years. It has recently been revived. I studied the beadwork of many cultures, particularly that of the Egyptians and of the Ojibway and Cree Indians. I realized that without any formal art training, these native craftspeople employ all the formal principles of design and composition: balance, line and color, symmetry, patterning, and symbolism, based on their observation of plant and animal forms in nature. They do not reproduce a leaf precisely, but through design and color they suggest its essence. They are intuitive artists.

I illustrated a book on Iroquois history. I studied our traditional symbols and their meaning for the Iroquois: the wampum belt patterns, silver-work designs, and animals carved in bone or wood. The turtle is our central symbol, identified with the land. Another is the eagle, which, according to our lore, perched on top of our sacred pine tree to warn the people of approaching danger. I found myself drawn to these images, and they continued to appear in my work.

I saw beauty in all the old art forms, but I was not satisfied reproducing what had been done before. To avoid getting stale, the artist must bring his own inventiveness to a pre-existing form. My style evolved, a contemporary statement, although it reflects my classical training and borrows something from my Indian heritage.

I'm basically a modernist. I love Matisse's cut-paper works and the special effects created by Rauschenberg: his use of nontraditional materials like cardboard, printing techniques, assemblage, and montage.

I began experimenting with different textural and color relationships.  I pushed paint through cloth, and when it dried, it left on the canvas patterns suggesting fish and bird forms.  I did a painting of the surface of a cantaloupe, with raised areas and lines dividing it into canals, and again, without conscious intent on my part, similar bird and animal forms appeared.

I continually observed plant forms in their natural environment. One that had always intrigued me was the sandburr, part of a plant that grows wild on our reservation.  I remember as a kid that if

Peter Jemison, *Sandburr*.  Acrylic, 1973.  Artist's collection.

you touched it, you got hurt.  There is a hard central core; from this core, sharp, piercing spikes radiate.  In my painting, I blew it up, stylized the shape, painted the spikes in varying shades of brown and rust, suggesting the different colors of Indian people. That was in 1973, the year Indians from tribes all over the United States occupied the town of Wounded Knee, South Dakota.  They were calling for self-determination, an end to federal intervention in reservation government.  FBI agents and marshals came in with high-powered rifles, machine guns, and armored personnel carriers, and blockaded the town.  It was a siege.  The sandburr became a symbol for me of Indian people joining together, using force because they believed that was the only way to regain control of their lives.

Self-determination is a critical issue for Indian people today. There are two Seneca reservations in New York State.  One, the Tonowanda band, has maintained the traditional form of government, with a hereditary chief appointed by the Clan Mothers and a Council of Chiefs that makes all decisions.  They're totally self-governing.  They refused to accept payment from the United States Claims Commission for land ceded in treaties, because they don't want the government interfering in tribal affairs.

In contrast, my reservation takes an expedient position.  We have an election every two years.  We negotiate with Washington and distribute government funds according to the regulations.  We work with the system.  But sometimes I wonder who really is in control.

I did another painting at the time of the Longest Walk in 1978. Indians were marching across the country to Washington to demand that the government honor long-standing treaties with the tribes.  My painting is a satirical comment.  It shows the paradox of the Statue of Liberty welcoming strangers to our shores, while turning her back on her own people.

My work is not political.  I'm not an activist.  And yet I cannot separate my art from my convictions.

In New York City, we are continually bombarded with information, new products, everything to satisfy our worldly needs.  To

Peter Jemison, *Riderless Horse*. Acrylic, 1978. Artist's collection.

regain my spiritual identity, I find I have to return home. This weekend I will participate in fall ceremonies on the Seneca Reservation. I will join with friends, sing and dance, smell the food cooking, listen to speeches. I'll thank the Creator for my family and for all the help I've had in this world. There is a time for repentance, for renewal of our beliefs, for looking forward. A speaker will recite the code of Handsome Lake.

In the early nineteenth century, this Seneca holy man called on all human beings to live according to the Great Law of the Iroquois, to live in peace. He foretold a time when men would not heed his counsel, when fires would come to the earth and trees would wither. Now, as nuclear accidents threaten our environment and our very existence, his words seem prophetic.[18]

# George Morrison,
## Ojibway/Chippewa painter and sculptor

*Ojibway people believe that in the mythical past, they came from the earth. Their life they perceive as a quest for unity with the natural world. After death, life continues in a new form.*

George Morrison prefers not to be rigidly classified as an "Indian artist." Because of his broad perspective, he thinks of himself as an artist who is Indian. He received formal art training at the Minneapolis School of Art, now the Minneapolis College of Art and Design, which many years later awarded him an honorary Master's Degree, and at the Art Students League in New York City.

In 1951, Morrison received a Fulbright fellowship to study and work in France, Italy, and Spain. This experience, along with the twenty years he spent living and working in the heart of the abstract movement in New York City, molded him artistically. In 1959, he entered the academic world and is now professor of studio arts at the University of Minnesota.

Despite urban influences, Morrison's art is firmly rooted in rural values — "more in earth than concrete," in the words of one critic. Recognized for its uniqueness and ingenuity, it is exhibited in this country's major collections. His cedar mural based on an Ojibway feather motif was specially designed for the front of the Minneapolis Regional Native American Center. A dramatic polychrome wood collage is on display at the Daybreak Star Arts Center in Seattle.

An Ojibway man, the elders taught, searches for a vision that *gives purpose and direction to his life. As he ages, he grows in wisdom. Philosophically, George Morrison shares the world view of his ancestors.*

═══
━━━

I was born in 1919 in Chippewa City, a small village near the Grand Portage Reservation in Minnesota. This was a heavily wooded area near Lake Superior. There were twelve children in our family, crowded into a small frame house without electricity or plumbing. We were often hungry and sick.

In my first year, I was at times carried by my mother in a cradleboard made by my father from cedar and cushioned with moss. I was wrapped in buckskin or cloth decorated with beadwork by my mother. This swaddling of the baby kept it warm and out of trouble, and supposedly held back, arms, and legs straight. I suppose there were psychological reasons too. It's a practice found among nomadic peoples, and even among the Russians. I suppose it was a way of controlling the young.

My father worked as an animal trapper for the government, and then later, when this became less lucrative and he could not provide for us, he became a laborer. He was fluent in the Chippewa language, which we spoke at home, and served as interpreter at court trials. When a priest was not available, he sang at funerals, wakes, and other ceremonies, translating English hymns into Chippewa. Eventually, he and my mother separated, and I was raised by my mother.

There was little left in those days of the old Indian art forms. A few people still made canoes and tipis out of birch bark. The women made beaded moccasins for special events. But most of the craft work was done for economic reasons. My grandmother carried on certain medicinal practices, using roots and herbs for healing. Like many older Indians, she didn't really trust the Health Service, and had more faith in the old folkways. Once her

George Morrison. Photo: Tom Foley. Courtesy University of Minnesota.

face became really twisted on one side. She was certain that this ugliness was brought about by an envious woman on the other side of the village. My grandmother experimented with roots and herbs and finally found an antidote to relieve the contortions, and they disappeared.

As I look back on my childhood, it was a time of transition. Indians had lost the best of the old world and could not fully cope with the new one. White civilization was encroaching on our lives. We attended white schools and were taught to imitate white people's ways. Our old mystical rites were no longer performed because they conflicted with church teachings. Our people viewed the church, I think, as a substitute for what they'd lost. People will take spiritual consolation wherever they can find it. Remnants of the old life survived, however. Fragments of the superstitions and lore I heard as a child stayed with me.

I attended Indian boarding school in Wisconsin. I had always worked with my hands — drawing, copying, and inventing — and was interested in commercial art. I began reading history and exploring art history, architecture, sculpture, and music. A scholarship to the Minneapolis School of Art gave me a sense of direction, for I obtained formal training in fine arts. I moved on to New York City, where I continued my studies, lived, and painted for the next twenty years. This was a time of great artistic ferment in New York, for the center of the art world had shifted there from Paris. The great abstract painters Mondrian, Feininger, and Max Ernst were there. I was exposed to a variety of styles, from cubism to surrealism to abstract expressionism.

The modern painters, particularly the cubists, were influenced by the art of tribal cultures. The tribal artist, whether African, Polynesian, Eskimo, or Indian, bases his art on his environment. He begins with organic shapes — animals, trees, mountains, the sun, the moon, for example. Zigzag lines may represent mountains, a round disc may signify the sun, but the forms are refined, stylized, even distorted, as each artist expresses his personal way of seeing. The ancient Egyptians created pyramidal structures based on geometric principles, which may have influenced the architecture of Central and South America. There are such similarities that one wonders about migratory patterns. All these ancient art forms reflect rich traditions and are powerful expressions. So-called primitive art can be very sophisticated.

I was soaking up inspiration from all these sources. My own style evolved slowly. I went through a semiabstract period, with human figures and landscape elements appearing in complex linear patterns. Even in my drawings of the simplest subject matter, there was a faint suggestion of organic forms: plants, water, clouds,

George Morrison, *Landscape II*. Wood collage, 1968. Courtesy Amon Carter Museum, Fort Worth, Texas.

animals, breasts, and limbs in the free-flowing curved lines. And
there was always a horizon line — a visible line separating earth
and sky. Surreal elements, images from the subconscious, began
to appear in my drawings and paintings.

In those early years I was interested in the Cubist technique of
breaking down landscape elements — a portion of land, water, or
sky — into sections, and I still work that way. Mosaic patterns appear frequently in my work, remotely suggesting Aztec art, perhaps
vaguely hinting at the complex weaving patterns of tribal peoples.
There's always been a preoccupation with textural surfaces. It's
evident in the scumbling, or overlaying of paint, in the paintings,
in the intricate crosshatchings and different thicknesses of lines in
the ink drawings, and in the wood surfaces of the collages. My
wood collages are made up of wood from the beaches of the Atlantic Coast and the shores of Lake Superior. I've always been attracted to the shore. I walk the beach searching for fragments of
wood that have interesting shape and texture, some with old ox-
idized nail holes showing. I let the wood age in my studio until it
has a grayish look, like a crusty old rock weathered by the elements
over a long period of time. I'm creating the illusion of something
that is old. What is art if not the creation of an illusion?

I don't use any preservatives, for they change the character of
the wood, and I prefer its natural surface. I accept the fact that
these wood structures will eventually decay. Change is inevitable,
a natural process. The most avant-garde work — a Frank Lloyd
Wright building, for example — becomes obsolete over a period
of time. The old gives way to the new. There's no guarantee of
immortality.

Recently I've been working on vertical structures, which resemble totem poles only in that they are vertical and have markings.
They have a carved appearance, but the technique is actually mosaic appliqué. I design individual pieces of wood according to a
formal pattern; each is glued onto a plywood core. I stain the
wood earth-red to give it potency and an Indian feeling. People
say that these works are reminiscent of the monumental structures
of Mexico's ancient Olmec peoples. I'm not sure whether the in-

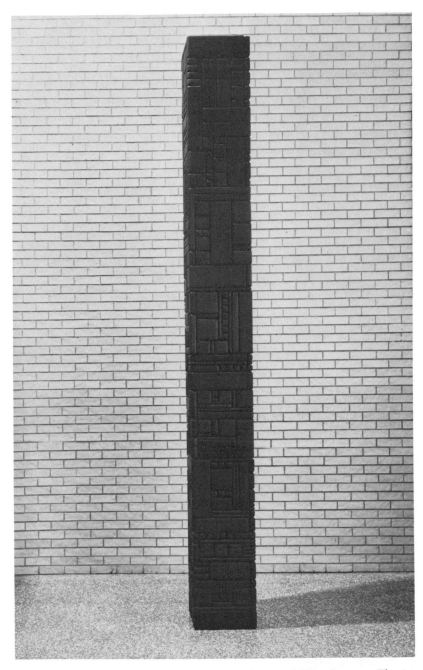

George Morrison, *Red Totem I*. Redwood with stain, 1977. Courtesy The Art Institute of Chicago.

fluence is conscious or unconscious, but I'm excited by the idea of reincarnating an art form that existed a thousand years ago.

I'm not religious in the usual sense. My art is my religion. I've tried to unravel the fabric of my life and how it relates to my work. Certain Indian values are inherent — an inner connection with the people and all living things, a sense of being in tune with natural phenomena, a consciousness of sea and sky, space and light, the enigma of the horizon, the color of the wind. I've never tried to prove my Indianness through my art. And yet there remains deep within some remote suggestion of the earth and the rock from which I came.[19]

# 4  From the Plains

*I will send a voice*
*to the Spirit of the World.*

### Black Elk

On grass-covered prairies west of the Mississippi, nomadic Plains Indians indulged their love of open spaces. Their altars were the rocks, the hills, the trees and streams entrusted to them by the Great Spirit. For religious and aesthetic reasons, they decorated the objects used in their daily life, their art proclaiming their individuality.

The warrior's shield was a banner, a testimony to his power and visionary experience, and a talisman that, if used according to custom, would protect him in battle. It was typically made of buffalo rawhide trimmed with trade cloth and feathers. On some shields, painted designs represented animals, birds, sacred mountains, and the sun and moon. When wars with the white man brought the Plains tribes to their knees, the shield lost its "medicine" or spiritual power, but it remained a central symbol in Plains art.

From red pipestone found in Minnesota and the Missouri River region, carvers fashioned the sacred pipes used on ceremonial occasions, often decorated with animals and birds. Ornamental headdresses were trimmed with feathers, horns, and weasel skins. Vessels and bags were made from rawhide and bear and elk skins. Clothing was made of buckskin, decorated by the women with fringes, shells, teeth, quills, and beads, mostly in geometric patterns.  The patterns were inspired by the motion in nature: the growth of crops, the flight of an arrow, rain, lightning.  Plains art was pictorial.  The artist translated personal experience into visual images understood by the group.

Tipis were decorated with symbols representing earth, stars, and animals, with figures from visions and dreams, and with geometric forms.  On hides, in an art form known as the Winter Count, Plains artists documented events in tribal history and individual exploits.  These "paintings" were actually ceremonial "happenings," in which community members participated on the long winter evenings.  They also functioned as tribal calendars before there was a written language.  The artists employed tribal symbols, stylized forms, and colors drawn from earth, plants, and trees.  Colors had symbolic significance, red standing for fire or blood, yellow for spirituality, blue for peace, and green for the growth of flora.  Dark areas suggested evil; light represented purity.

After their defeat, Plains people were imprisoned behind wire fences, but their creative spirit would not be confined.  On notebooks supplied by their captors, they drew the scenes of their childhood, remembered battles and impressions of wounded bodies.  The art of these prisoners of war is remarkable for its sharply drawn lines, detail, and representational style.

Plains art evolved over the years.  The artists departed from convention in their use of line and color.  The symbols were modified, and abstract elements tended to replace representational.  Oscar Howe, Sioux/Dakotah, often considered the founder of the contemporary Indian art movement writes: "I experienced a creative sense as a child in my first lines of drawing, but I remember such drawings were complete abstractions and not Indian abstract symbols or recognizable objects.  I thought my first lines were beautiful, plastic, and full of tension; I even sensed live quality in them.  I remember my parents saw these lines and told me never to draw them again.  I still made these lines when no one was watching — three-dimensional lines in space, but they appeared two-dimensional, so I had to imagine them moving in and out of space . . ."[20]  Howe's painting, he explains, is closely associated with Dakotah experience and gains its direction, purpose, and substance from traditional Dakotah art.

The younger generation of Plains artists has been influenced by the art of their ancestors. Although today's styles tend toward abstraction and innovation, the artist may incorporate such materials as feathers, fur, bark, and quills, and may use traditional motifs, giving them new life. Among the more notable of the contemporary Plains artists is Robert Penn, Sioux, an abstract painter.

# Amos Owen,
## Sioux/Dakotah pipe-carver

*Among the Sioux elders it is said that many years ago from out of a cloud came a sacred woman, White Buffalo Calf Woman, and that to a Sioux chief she gave a pipe with a bison calf carved on one side and twelve eagle feathers hanging from the stem. And she said, "Behold. With this pipe you shall multiply and be a good nation."* [21]

When Amos Owen smokes his sacred peace pipe, meticulously carved out of pipestone found deep within the earth's surface, he is invoking the spirits of earth and sky, mingling his breath with the wind, the breath of the universe. It is therefore ironic that just a mile down the road from the Amos Owen house on Sioux reservation land in Minnesota is the Prairie Island nuclear plant which, its opponents say, is defiling that sacred earth and air. (On October 3, 1979, there was a nuclear accident at the plant, and radiation was released into the air.) Owen's land has been the site of protest demonstrations designed to close down the nuclear plant. A former tribal chairman, he feels a responsibility to the earth, to his people, and to future generations.

Through the pipe ceremony, Owen expresses a sense of the brotherhood of all peoples. "We use the pipe not only for the pleasure of smoking, but to share with others," he says. The pipe may be decorated with feathers, the eagle feather representing the independence and strength of the Sioux nation. In ages past, the *pipemakers used flint to hollow out the bowl, they smoothed the pipe with sandstone and polished it with buffalo tallow. Owen uses an electric drill, sandpaper, and beeswax for polishing.*

*Owen grew up in Sisseton, South Dakota. A Marine Corps veteran of World War II, he has worked as a packing-house employee, a commercial fisherman, and a deputy game warden. In the movie* The Immigrants, *which was filmed in Wisconsin, he made a brief appearance as a Plains Indian on horseback.*

*Owen has taught the art of pipe-carving in the public schools of Minnesota and the Dakotas. On commission, he has carved peace pipes for the governor of Minnesota and the chancellor of Austria, and he has been sent by the United States Information Agency to Budapest, Hungary, to demonstrate carving and the way of the pipe.*

. . . I know that it is a good thing I am going to do; and because no good thing can be done by any man alone, I will first make an offering and send a voice to the Spirit of the World, that it may help me to be true. See, I fill this sacred pipe with the bark of the red willow . . .

Sioux holy man Black Elk to John Neihardt, 1931[21]

My name is Wiyohpeyata-Hoksina. I am of the Dakotah tribe. I speak and write in the Dakotah language.

My father was a half-breed. His mother was from Sitting Bull's band. Chaska was his Indian name. He was a farmer and kept horses, and I had my own horse from the time I could walk. My mother was full-blooded, from the Sisseton-Wahpeton branch of the Eastern Sioux, a member of Chief Wabasha's band. They settled in this big white house on Sioux Reservation land in Prairie Island, Minnesota. After our marriage, my wife Ione and I moved in with them. We raised our seven children here.

Amos Owen.  Photo: Randy Croce.

As a boy, I drew and painted.  I went to school in Pipestone, Minnesota.  That's the site of the Pipestone Quarries, where Indians from all tribes gather to quarry the sacred stone used by their ancestors for countless generations.  There, historically, the Indians laid down their weapons and worked side by side in harmony — a United Nations of all tribes.  I watched the old Sioux men carve and learned from them. At first it was a hobby, and I gave the pipes away, but then orders began coming in from all over the world — from Germany, France, and the Scandinavian countries — and now it's full-time work. Every summer I return to Pipestone to quarry the stone. The quarry is sacred ground. I make my offerings before I go.

Obtaining the stone is difficult work. There's a thick outer covering of rock, called quartzite, which you have to break up with a sledgehammer. It may take days to get down to the vein of pipestone below, which you then pry loose and haul out with pincher bars, trying to keep the slab intact.

Back at home, I say a prayer with the stone, asking the spirits to guide my hands while I carve the stone. I work out in my backyard. Often I hear a screeching noise and look up to see four eagles circling over my head. It's a good feeling to know that the spirits are with me. I draw a design freehand on the stone, then cut it out with a hacksaw. For fine carving, I use rat-tail files. The surface of the stone has to be really smooth. The base of the bowl of the pipe is squared off, the rest is rounded. The T-shaped pipe is traditional. Often, I sculpt a buffalo onto the pipe, a symbolic tribute to the animal that once provided for us, or the head of an eagle. I carve a band around the bowl — that's my trademark.

The stem of the pipe is most often made of sumac. There's a grove of sumac trees growing in the valley near here. I think of it as my own special place, for no one else goes there. I wander through the grove searching for a tree that is slightly bent. My pipestems all have a curved wooden stem, like a tree bending in the wind, leaning over as if it's getting ready to die. I never cut green wood, for I would not destroy growing timber. Sumac has a short growth cycle — only five or six years — and although the tree is still standing, it's dried out inside and already dead when I cut it. I only cut what I need. I spray the pipestem with pure acrylic. That brings out the grain and preserves the wood. It's beautiful that way.

The stem fits into the bowl of the pipe. It must be centered,

and I use an electric drill to make the hole — my one concession
to modern technology. The pipes break easily, but I've only had
one pipe break. It was my fault. I was in a hurry, started working
without prayers, and when I used the electric drill, the stone shat-
tered. If the pipe is made properly, the stone will last forever.

The Sioux have always carved. In earlier times, a holy woman
gave us the pipe, with instructions as to how we should live.
Elkhead was the first Keeper of the Pipe. That's recorded in the
Winter Count. One man in a band was the official carver, chosen for his natural talent. And the old way, the way of the pipe,
came down to us.

I do a service every morning before sunrise. I pray heavenward,
then to the four directions of the universe, and then to Mother
Earth. When I pray to Mother Earth, I point the pipestem to the
earth. I pray for my family, for Indian people, and for all people.
I give thanks for each sunrise and for being able to live to see
another day in all its beautiful colors.

We believe in the circle of life. As I begin the pipe ceremony, I
point the pipe to the West, for this is where the Sun goes down.
I pray to Wakinyan — the Thunder Beings. I pray to Waziya —
the North, for the healing wind that comes from the North. I
pray to the East, to the Morning Star that gives us wisdom. The
pipe comes from the East. I pray to the South, from where all
good things come — the spring of the year, green growing things,
warm winds.

Many of our people today pray to the Four Directions, to Creation. In our ceremonies, we smoke a substance called cansha-
sha. That is the inner bark of red willow mixed with tobacco.
The willow gives it an aroma. I add shavings of sweet flag, a wild
herb that grows in the marshes. Some people use bloodroot. The
herbs are believed to help with breathing problems, especially
asthma.

I'm not a medicine man or healer, but I'm often called on to
perform the pipe ceremony for our people at weddings, give-away
ceremonies, family reunions, and memorial services. My son
Raymond, who is an apprentice pipe-carver, assists and serves as

pipe-bearer. While I concentrate on prayers for the people who have requested the ceremony, he prepares the pipe, lights it, and passes it around so that all can smoke. Once a year, before a ceremony, I fast to honor the spirits of my ancestors. I take no food or drink or tobacco for twenty-four hours.

Once my nephew was in an auto accident and had severe hip pain. He asked me to say prayers with the pipe. During the ceremony, he started shaking — it really reached him. Afterward, he said he never felt so good in his life, and he's had no more trouble. I don't believe I did anything, but the spirits are looking after him.

The pipe has meaning for our people today. They're going back to ceremony, to the way of the pipe. The pipe provides guidance, shows us a way of life. When I do a ceremony at an Indian school, even though the children don't understand the Dakotah language, they know I'm praying to the Four Directions, and they pray along with me in their hearts. They feel the presence of the Great Spirit.

Raymond and I took part in the Longest Walk, when Indian people from all over the country marched to Washington, D.C., to demand recognition of our treaty rights. We conducted pipe ceremonies there.

A few years ago, I camped with my young son in Shakopee, Minnesota, which used to be a Sioux settlement. That's our homeland. It's rich in Indian lore. There are the burial mounds of our ancestors all around. We cooked over a fire, then put food out for the spirits — that's the tradition. Eagles hovered about. That was the first time our people had returned to that area, and I think the spirits were welcoming us.

Another time, in Mankato, the place where thirty-eight Sioux were hanged in 1862 for their part in an uprising against the U.S. Army, we held a powwow in a ball park. We formed a circle and staged a grand entry into the arena. We heard the screeching of eagles, and saw them circling overhead. The Medicine Man said there were thirty-eight eagles — one for each warrior who had died. After 111 years, the Sioux had finally come back.

Black Elk was the great Holy Man of the Lakotah, the Western Sioux.* In the twilight of his years, he went to the highest mountain. With what little power he had left, he prayed to the Thunder Beings, and in a little while it rained. I believe that all his prophecies are true for the Dakotah, except one. He said that the sacred tree, symbolic of all trees, died because men were not true to his vision. I don't see it that way. When I carve a pipe-stem out of the sacred tree used by my ancestors, I feel I'm keeping it alive.

The Thunder Beings come out of the West. They control thunder, lightning, rain. When we travel, we place the pipe on the dashboard of our car, and they watch over us on our way home, ensuring our personal safety. It makes me feel that I'm somebody special to know that they're watching over me. It's a presence. I know it's there.[22]

---

* Dakotah refers to the Eastern Sioux, or to the entire Sioux Nation.

# 5 From the Southwest

*We had no teachers. We knew how to paint by ourselves. It was as if we remembered our paintings, as if they had come before us like the plants from out of the ground.*

Fred Kabotie, Hopi

In the southwestern United States, ancient mountains preside over arid plateaus; red sandstone buttes rise above flat, dry mesas; rock-walled canyons are carved into low-lying deserts and river valleys. A wide variety of art forms flourish among Southwest Indian tribes, some existing in an unbroken continuum since prehistoric times, others representing a revival of once lost arts.

The architectural skills of Indian people can be seen in the prehistoric dwelling places unearthed by archeologists in excavation sites in Arizona and New Mexico. With great ingenuity, early peoples built cliff houses into the steep stone walls of the Puye Cliffs area near Santa Fe. In a later period, many-storied "apartment houses" were constructed out of adobe or sun-baked clay in the pueblos of New Mexico and Arizona. Not only are these dwellings picturesque, but their solid construction has enabled them to survive the centuries.

On the walls of caves, cliff dwellings, and the great rock canyons of the Southwest can be found remnants of the pictographs and petroglyphs of prehistoric native peoples. In colorful pictorial symbols, the ancestors of present-day Indian tribes recorded daily activities, their view of the cosmos, and their relationship to the all-pervasive spirit of the natural world on which they believed their survival depended. These drawings had a ceremonial purpose. One didn't have to reproduce the subject precisely; the drawing contained the subject's spirit and its power: "The germ of the corn plant or the life of the entire field might be concentrated in a dot within a rectangular enclosure. The increase of the herd might be ensured by clearly drawing the breath-of-life line on a schematic form indicating the body of the deer . . ."[23]

The "breath of life" is the wind, the breathing of the universe. It is a part of the life force and is thus associated by Indians with creation, the growth of human and animal life. The mountain, the cloud, the lightning, the corn plant — each had its symbol, identifiable by the group. Colors, derived from charcoals, minerals, and vegetal substances, might indicate one's tribe or clan, the season or time of day, and one's magical purpose. One color was identified with life and growth, another with evil and destruction.

Excavations of ancient Pueblo* sites, such as those at Awatovi in the Hopi area of Northeastern Arizona, and Kuaua and Pottery Mound, both near Albuquerque, New Mexico, uncovered elaborate paintings adorning the walls of kivas, semiunderground ceremonial chambers of the Anasazi people, a prehistoric civilization that reached its peak in the thirteenth century. Anasazi achievements in weaving and pottery were impressive. Their religious life centered around agriculture and the use of kachinas or effigies to invoke spirits. Copies were made of these great wall frescoes (which had begun to fade once exposed to the air), thus preserving the art and heritage of the Anasazi. The kiva murals contain colorful symbols, sacred objects, and mythological figures that testify to the rich ceremonial life of one of the world's great civilizations. In the history of Southwest Indian painting, rock art and kiva murals are important, for these early works introduced many of the visual symbols and painting conventions that were to influence profoundly the work of modern Indian artists.

Another early art form that has inspired contemporary Indian

---

* Pueblo is capitalized when it refers to Southwest tribes descended from the ancient Anasazi people: the Hopi of northeastern Arizona, the Zuni of western New Mexico, and the many tribes of New Mexico's Rio Grande Valley, among them San Ildefonso, Santa Clara, Taos, San Juan, Santo Domingo, Acoma, and Laguna.

artists is sand painting, or dry painting. Navajos, relatively late arrivals in the Southwest, learned this technique from the Pueblo Indians, but developed and perpetuated it. Sand painting is the work of a Navajo medicine man who, to heal bodily or spiritual ills, pictures symbolically the yeis, or deities, and the complex religious beliefs of these once nomadic people. Because of their sacred nature, the "paintings" are destroyed after use, but their subject matter and graphic images have been reproduced symbolically by painters and weavers.

From earliest times, Indians painted on every available material: on hides, bark, wood, and bone, in addition to rock and house walls. Pueblo men painted designs on the pottery made by the women. But instruction was not programmed. The child learned within the extended family by watching and experimenting.

Kiva mural, *The Squash Maiden and Warrior*. Awatovi Ruins, Hopi Mesas, Arizona. Courtesy Museum of the American Indian, Heye Foundation.

The modern school of American Indian painting began in the Southwest in the first two decades of the twentieth century with the work of Crescencio Martinez of San Ildefonso Pueblo, a brother-in-law of the world-famous potter Maria. Without any formal training in art, Martinez moved from the decoration of pottery to the creation of stylized watercolors depicting Pueblo dancers and drummers in their winter and summer ceremonies.

Another self-taught artist, one of a group of young painters who were students at the Santa Fe Indian School was the Hopi, Fred Kabotie. Kabotie recorded, with great precision and skill in draftsmanship, the formal pattern of Hopi ceremonials, particularly the kachina dancers (masked figures who are believed to embody the spirits of Pueblo deities) and scenes from everyday Pueblo life. Dorothy Dunn writes: "His performers are not men dressed as gods: they are gods. Perhaps nowhere in the work of the modern Indian artists is the man-to-supernatural link, as interpreted by ceremonial impersonation, conveyed with such conviction as in Kabotie's art. Symbolic realism transcends representationalism — far and away — and painting becomes as persuasive as the dancers in life . . . They are filled with vitality and potential action, emanating power . . ."[24]

During the same period, a group of young Kiowa artists, descendants of a plains tribe that was resettled in Oklahoma after the defeat of the Indian nations, had been brought together by Susan Peters of the United States Indian Service in Anadarko, Oklahoma, and was achieving some prominence. Their work was highly decorative and stylized, filled with action and animation. The subject matter was nostalgic, focusing mainly on tribal ceremonies, such as the War Dance, Hoop and Feather Dances, and the rituals of the peyote cult. Recognition given the Santa Fe and Kiowa artists provided impetus for Indian artists throughout the Southwest, and there were exhibitions of Indian art at some of the nation's leading museums.

In the years 1932–1937, classes taught by Dorothy Dunn at the Studio, the Art Department of the Santa Fe Indian School, exposed young Indians to the art of the great Indian civilizations.

Pablita Velarde, *The Emergence of the Tewa*. Casein. Indian Pueblo Cultural Center, Albuquerque. Photo: Edwin B. Nelson, Jr.

Students gathered natural materials — clay, sandstones, and color-bearing ores and minerals — from which they learned to produce watercolors and temperas. They depicted the clouds, terraced mountains, and plumed serpents found on wall paintings and ancient pottery, at the same time creating their own variations of old motifs. A "Studio style" evolved, often described as flat, decorative, pictorial, typified by the work of Santa Clara artist Pablita Velarde, who has devoted a lifetime to recording scenes from everyday Indian life and the religious and political life of Pueblo people. In casein tempera and oils, using for the most part muted earth tones, Velarde paints the costumes, rituals, lore, and symbolism of her people with knowledge and precision.

By the late 1930s, the Indian artist had been "discovered" by whites. This led to commercialism as Indian art became a profitable commodity, with imitative and stereotyped painting, such as the "Bambi school" — a proliferation of deer prancing over purple mountains.

Since the 1960s, Indian artists have moved away from tradi-

tional styles and conventional subject matter.  They have absorbed
influences from contemporary European and Oriental art and explored the realm of the avant-garde.  They have succeeded in in-
corporating what is of value in other traditions without diluting
their own.

New artists have come forward.  Fritz Scholder, a painter who
is one-quarter Mission/Luiseno Indian, is in the foreground of this
"new wave."  His subtly ironic studies of contemporary Indians

Fritz Scholder, *Indian, Rifle, and Horse.*  Oil, 1979.  Courtesy of the artist.

are starkly individualistic, tending toward caricature. A former student of Oscar Howe, trained in abstract expressionism and pop art, he portrays Indians, cowboys, and women with distorted faces and figures, suggesting the paradoxical condition of their lives. Scholder views painting as a "highly sensual act":

> I like large canvases, a brush that is pliable, buttery paint, dramatic line and color. I establish a physical relationship with the canvas and engage in a silent battle. The process is free association and an explosion of energy. The result may be a disaster. More often, it's a victory.
>
> I reject the visual cliché of the noble savage bending over a fire sharpening his arrows. My buffalo dancer may wear traditional garb, but he'll hold an ice-cream cone or a beer can. I have depicted the Bureau of Indian Affairs as a rhinoceros.
>
> I try to capture not only the physical aspect of a subject, but its soul or spirit.[25]

Many art forms found within the caves and subterranean chambers of the ancients have survived or have been revived by contemporary tribal people. In the pueblos along the Rio Grande and on the mesas, one can find today outstanding examples of the weaver's art, basketry, pottery and clay figurines, mosaic work and the lapidary arts, handcrafted silver and turquoise jewelry, and wooden kachinas. Allan Houser has been in the foreground of the field of sculpture, a recent development in the Southwest.

Change, growth, innovation — these are the bywords of the Indian artists of the Southwest. And yet one facet of their work is immutable — its deeply spiritual quality, for it is rooted in profound religious convictions that unite all the tribes. There is balance and harmony in the art, reflecting the belief in an ordered, structured universe and in the interrelatedness of all phenomena, whether spiritual, inanimate, human, or animal. Human beings exist in an intimate relationship to the earth, which is alive and breathing. Natural forces are portrayed animistically, and spiritual beings often take human form.

In a recent visit to a retrospective exhibit of the work of five generations of her family, the potter Maria Martinez — in a wheelchair at age ninety-five — visited each pot on display, touching it lovingly. Her great-granddaughter Barbara Gonzales, also a potter, said the family always greets pots this way: "The pots for us, you see, are people — our children perhaps. They have gender. Some are called women. Some are men. And they have personalities. The pots seem to be doing different things. So when we haven't seen a pot for a long time, well, it's like an old friend who has to be greeted and examined to be sure she hasn't suffered in the meantime. We remember our pots, though they have gone far away."[26]

*Song of the Sky Loom*

*Oh our Mother the Earth, oh our Father the Sky,*
*Your children are we, and with tired backs*
*We bring you the gifts that you love.*
*Then weave for us a garment of brightness;*
*May the warp be the white light of morning,*
*May the weft be the red light of evening,*
*May the fringes be the falling rain,*
*May the border be the standing rainbow.*
*Thus weave for us a garment of brightness*
*That we may walk fittingly where the birds sing . . .*[27]

# Pearl Sunrise,
# Navajo weaver and basketmaker

*The Navajo people view themselves as inextricably bound to the sacred earth, from which they believe their ancestors came in an earlier time. The materials used in their weaving have traditionally come from the earth — wool from Navajo sheep, dyes from wild plants and berries, the vertical loom from tree trunks held in place by rocks. Their blankets provided a link between the material and spiritual worlds: "When the Navajo wrapped blankets around themselves, they were surrounding their bodies with the totality of their being, gathering about themselves the four corners of a world at once beautiful and familiar . . . In their blankets, the Navajo had a visual language that enabled them to show each other who they were. The blankets were self-portraits in which the Navajo manifested their place among people, their integration with the landscape, and their oneness with the spiritual forces of life."* [28]

*In the last generation, the lifestyle of the Navajo weaver has changed radically. Most have given up the pastoral existence of sheepherders and have moved to commercial centers where processed wools and dyes, as well as markets, are readily available, thus increasing productivity and income. They have exchanged their hogan for the white man's house. They have accepted the pickup truck and TV as facts of modern life. But their dedication to the art of their ancestors remains unchanged.*

*Pearl Sunrise is an award-winning weaver and weaving instruc-
tor. She lives with her family in Albuquerque, New Mexico.*

━━━━

I was born in the forties when the North Star was midway across
the sky. We lived then in an adobe home in Whitewater, New
Mexico, on the eastern part of the Navajo Reservation. My pater-
nal grandfather's name was Pintohorse, and so I was named Pearl
Pintohorse or granddaughter of Pintohorse — Gleh-Dez-Bah in
Navajo. There was much rejoicing at my birth, for my parents
had lost two children. The ceremonies and prayers were elaborate.

My parents were sheepherders and had no formal education.
My mother wove rugs and made clothing. Father made jewelry
and was an astrologist. He studied the stars in the night sky,
predicted the weather and approaching storms. My maternal
grandparents lived in a hogan on another part of the reservation.
Wrapped in shawls, their fine black hair combed back into the
traditional Navajo knot, they'd come on horseback to visit us.
They'd bring the ripe squash, watermelons, and peaches they'd
harvested, and the lovely rugs and shawls Grandmother wove.
Grandfather prayed throughout the day. We children sat with
him, combing his hair and tying it into a knot, waiting for the
stories he always told.

Spider woman, he said, taught the Navajo women how to
weave. Spider Man taught them how to make the loom. The
cross-poles were formed from sky and earth cords, the warp sticks
from sun rays, rock crystal, and sheet lightning. The batten was a
sun halo, the comb a white shell. When this, the Fourth World
was set up, Spider Woman wove the earth into a tapestry of natural colors and beautiful designs. [In the beginning, according to
Navajo and Pueblo cosmology, the people lived in several worlds
below the earth and emerged in successive stages to this world.]

Pearl Sunrise. Photo: Bill Sunrise.

As a child I was very quiet. I listened intently to everything the elders taught. I was busy observing the world around me.

We all helped with the chores. My brothers, my sisters, and I chopped wood. We cared for the cattle and rode horses. I helped Mother shear the sheep, and using cards — wooden boards with metal teeth — we combed the rough wool into fine strands. When I was eight or nine, I began herding sheep. We lived in the country, isolated from everything. I led the sheep far out onto the hillside. At noon, when the sun was hot, I'd sit under a piñon tree, and the sheep would crowd around. Along with my lunch, mother always packed a bundle of wool, cards, and a spindle, and I did my carding and spinning there. It was peaceful.

In those days, Navajo girls wore long skirts with high-topped brown shoes — not the most comfortable outfit for sheepherding, so I often changed into my brothers' Levi's. That was a hard thing for my parents to accept.

When I was still quite young, and despite my parents' objections, I was sent far from home to a Bureau of Indian Affairs boarding school. I deeply resented being taken from my family. We were taught by white people who knew nothing of our culture. They lined us up, marched us around, and it was like being in the army. We were ordered to speak English, the universal language, but this was very difficult, for first we had to translate the words we heard back into Navajo to make sense of them, then we had to learn a whole new vocabulary and speech pattern. When we spoke Navajo, we were punished, for our language was supposedly inferior, and so we could barely communicate with each other. I felt very much alone.

My father had always taught us to wear our hair long in the traditional Navajo way, but the school tried to transform us quickly into "whites." And when I returned home with my hair chopped off, wearing jeans, with my name anglicized to Pinto, he whipped me.

I returned to the familiar pattern of Navajo life. I learned to weave, to do basketry, to make clothing and jewelry from my parents and aunts. I won recognition for my weaving, and my tribe provided a scholarship for me to study fine arts at the University of New Mexico. There I got involved in drawing, painting, and sculpture. Now I'm working toward an M.A. in art education, so that I can teach my own people.

There are so many things in our lifestyle that are better than what I see in the white man's world. In my weaving, as in other things, I'm very traditional. I think it's because of the blessings I received at my birth. Those who have gone before me into the spirit world are guiding me.

Most weavers today use commercial wool and dyes, but I think chemicals are dangerous. I use raw wool and natural dyes. Cochineal red comes from a bug found in Mexico — I trade with a man for it. The brown and black dyes come from wild walnut shells and mountain mahogany, the yellow from sagebrush. I go with my family into the Sandia Mountains to gather the plants. Before taking anything from the earth, we ask permission. We pray to the Creator: "With beauty surrounding me in four directions — East, South, West and North, you've made this place beautiful for me. You've made the sky, the stars, the plants, everything in nature. I'm taking some of these plants to use in my work. Make it good for me. With beauty surrounding me to the East, South, West, and North." We are careful not to take more than we need, to conserve the plants for others.

When I prepare the wool — there are many steps in a very complicated process — I again pray to the Creator for skill. When I weave, I experiment. I have my own personal style, but my designs are all variations of old designs, using traditional symbols and geometric forms. My favorite is the storm pattern with clouds and lightning surrounding a hogan; I add cornstalks in the spring or summer.

I make baskets, too. These are used in our healing ceremonies, and they're too expensive to buy in the trading posts. We gather the plants in the hills of the Durango Colorado mountains. My people used to go there in groups on horseback to gather sumac for baskets, so I do it in the same way. We pray to the Creator before taking the plants. I use only one pattern, depicting clouds, a rainbow, and the four Sacred Mountains. Only after I made my first basket was I permitted to hear our creation story. After emerging from the lower world, it is said, the people gathered at a great rock at the center of the earth and planted seeds to make the earth spread out. Then they called on the Holy People to help plant the four Sacred Mountains. These still surround our homeland.

I made the dress I'm wearing and my jewelry. I was born into so many arts, but weaving is what I prefer. It gives me a sense of serenity. [29]

*O the colors, Grandmother,*
*I saw in the two-days-ago rainbow.*

*O Grandmother Spider, the sun is shining*
*through your loom.*

*She works gently, her skirt flared out,*
*in the sun of this morning's Summer . . .*[30]

                              Simon Ortiz

# Mary Morez,
## Navajo painter

*Instinct, intuition, and faith intertwine in the complex lore and ceremonials of the Navajo. From the dark place of beginning in Mother Earth, human beings emerge and begin their ascent toward their father, the Sky. Along "the Way," or the Road of Life, they seek to master instincts and "evil" thoughts from the dark unconscious. The goal is an ethical life. One must live in harmony with the earth, the mountains, the "house of dark cloud and evening twilight."*

*From her early years on the Navajo Reservation, Mary Morez derived a sense of the miracle and mystery of life and an interest in Navajo history and religion. After graduation from the University of Arizona and the Ray Vogue Art School, she served as research associate at the Heard Museum in Phoenix, and as staff consultant to the Museum of Navajo Ceremonial Art in Santa Fe.*[31] *In 1969, she embarked on a career in painting and graphics.*

*While her subjects are most often topically Indian, depicting both traditional and modern life, the context is universal. In vivid colors and a striking, impressionistic style, she depicts dream images, mythological figures, and symbols from Navajo lore and sand painting. This has led to increasing abstraction as she explores the symbolism of one culture using the media and techniques of another.*

My art is a way of reaching out to people, of confronting the barriers between them.   People are fascinating.   I work as a volunteer in a hospital.   Sometimes I see a fantastic face, really striking. I stare and stare, hoping no one will notice, then I start drawing. The face becomes the only reality for me.   The eyes burn at you beyond dimension.

I see such complexity and groping in some contemporary In-

Mary Morez, *The Face*.  Mixed media, 1977.

dians. It's really hard for them to get the old and the new together. If you've been brought up as an Indian and you move into Anglo society, you have to break through a psychological barrier that is unseen, only felt. You have to cross over from one world into another that is totally different in terms of environment, concept of life, religion. Once you come to realize who you are and establish an identity in both worlds, this barrier is broken and you can begin to feel comfortable. You can join together the two lifestyles, and you'll be much stronger.

I was born on the Navajo reservation in Tuba City, Arizona. My grandparents raised me there until I was five. They poured Navajo beliefs into me in the Navajo language. My grandfather used to say the human mind is like a sponge. He taught me to soak up knowledge and experience. They took me to the Navajo sings — there's great power in the singing, chanting, and prayers that are said for a patient who is physically ill. We believe that sickness of the body is caused by psychological sickness. The goal of the Navajo is to stay in tune with nature. If you're tense and anxious, you disrupt that harmony and bring sickness on yourself. A medicine man has the power to heal, using herbs and sweat baths. He prays over the patient in a lodge or hogan consecrated for this purpose. The night chant is serene and beautiful:

> *In the house made of dawn,*
> *In the house made of evening twilight,*
> *In the house made of dark cloud . . .*
> *With your headdress of dark cloud come to us,*
> *With your mind enveloped in dark cloud, come to us!*

The healer sprinkles pollen over the patient. He constructs a sand painting, a symbolic representation of the deities, and applies the sand to the patient's body. This all has a therapeutic effect; evil influences are released. My visual impressions of sand paintings are a way of getting closer to the unseen.

There is another part of the Night Chant that has special meaning for me. My grandparents used to say, "This is everybody's prayer. Use it when you feel downhearted":

Mary Morez. Photo: Dick Church.

> *Happily with abundant dark clouds may I walk.*
> *Happily on a trail of pollen may I walk . . .*
> *In beauty may I walk.*

You are taught to do whatever you have to do with serenity. You live the prayer. When anything goes wrong, you say these words to give yourself or someone else strength. Always you say the right thing at the right time to help another. You give your strength. The more you give, the more you get in return.

In beauty may I walk. That's my idea of family life. Men and women need each other, depend on each other. If you give love, you get love in return, without asking for it. Never ask for gratitude. Sometimes people call for help, and I try to respond. But you can't give so much that you're an empty vessel.

I was married to an Anglo archaeologist. We were of different backgrounds, different religions. Yet there was mutual understanding, a deep trust. He died a few years ago, a slow and painful death. When he was dying, he took our daughter Sheila outside and spoke to her of the stars, the trees, all the things he loved. He devoured life, especially when he knew he was dying, and he wanted us both to experience it as fully as he did. He gave us so much. His love is still a part of our lives.

You can't live for yourself. To be happy, you have to live for other human beings, for the land, the religion, the universe. Too many Anglos live for today. They have to have land, wealth, electricity, fuel, now. They contaminate the land and wildlife, the air and water. They don't think about what will happen to their grandchildren. I attend council meetings and conferences, and I say what I think. But most people don't like to hear the truth. I want my daughter and her children to grow up in a safe world.

For Indian people, children are so important. I think they are beautiful. They should remain children as long as possible. You should teach them, love them, give them your strength, share your life with them. In my paintings, I try to convey the close bond between mothers and children. I have painted my impressions of the yei, the spirit who is the guardian of the child, and of the yei who protects our home. Our home is the center of the sacred world. We bless a new home with cornmeal, for it's a beginning.

I depict these Navajo deities symbolically. My yei is a female goddess to fit all moods. I paint her in bright colors. That's life!

We have always learned from animals. I did a painting of Owl Woman, a figure from Navajo lore. The owl calls at a certain time of day. We believe it's a message, and you'd better be prepared for it.

I relive my dreams in my paintings. I can visit many places in

Mary Morez, *The Weaver's Yei*.  Oil, 1977.

my dreams.  I love to dance.  I wear a shawl when I go to dances, out of respect for the older people who don't like to see a woman un-covered.  I go to powwows, and paint the costumed dancers.  No matter how drab their lives might be, at the dances Indians come to life.  My paintings of dances are done in brilliant color in acrylic — it captures fast movement in color.

A woman is like an eagle, free and in motion.  My grandmother taught me that you can be feminine and still be strong. "A woman doesn't have much muscle," she said. "Use your brain instead. Use your heart. That's where the power comes from."

I've been going to school all my life. I've taken night classes. I've studied anthropology, psychology, and philosophy. Now I'm taking photography — it's another dimension of art. Going to school makes life exciting. I think I'll go to school until they put me away. I won't let anything hold me back.

I've read the Old Testament and the New Testament several times, trying to understand the difference between religions. I've come to the conclusion that human beings make their own religion. I believe in a supreme being, but we have to make our own rules, rules we can live with.

Navajo prayers are so very meaningful to me. They make you feel you're part of the trees, the plants, the flowers, the raindrops, the thunder, the dawn, the blackness that is night. My grandmother used to say, "Don't be afraid of the night. Just think that your grandmother moon is putting a blanket over you so you can sleep." She taught me not to fear death. It is part of the cycle. The sun goes down, the day ends; so with life. But life renews itself. This I tell my daughter, and she in turn will tell her daughter.

Grandmother taught me to respect the dead. But I don't believe in life after death. I live my life now, the way I want to live it. I like to think that if I live a good life, people will remember me. In that way, I will live on.[32]

Navajo Healing Ceremony


With the zigzag lightning flung over your head,
    come to us, soaring!
With the zigzag lightning flung out high on the
    ends of your wings, come to us soaring!
With the rainbow hanging high on the ends of your
    wings, come to us, soaring! . . .

Far off you have done it!
Happily I recover! [33]

# R. C. Gorman,
## Navajo painter, sculptor, and lithographer

R. C. Gorman first won attention for his artistic endeavors when on the dirt floor of the one-room school he attended in Chinle, Arizona, he drew the figure of a nude woman, and was promptly spanked. But his creativity wasn't stifled.

"Art has always been our way of life," he has said. "I am the descendant of sand painters, silversmiths, chanters, weavers, and probably, as rumored, talented witch doctors." Born Rudolph Carl Gorman, the son of artist Carl Nelson Gorman who broke with the traditional mold of Indian painting, he grew up on the Navajo Reservation near the historic Canyon de Chelly with its towering cliff walls and caves, once the dwelling place of the Anasazi, ancestors of the Navajo. Petroglyphs on the canyon's rock walls and stories of "the ancient ones" fired the imagination of the young Gorman, whose first ambition was to be a writer.

He majored in art and literature in college, then received a scholarship from the Navajo tribe to study mural painting in Mexico City, where he was inspired by the work of the great Mexican painters Rivera, Siqueiros, Orozco, and Tamayo. Gorman developed his own figurative style, characterized by elegant lines, flowing motion, and subtle pastels contrasting with vibrant colors. He is best known for his classic line drawings of Navajo women performing their daily chores and for his Navajo rug series, an attempt to give permanence to the rich textures and motifs of this exquisite art *form. His work encompasses a variety of media, including litho-graphs, serigraphs, etchings, ceramics, and bronzes.*

*Gorman has been described as "a transitional figure outside the pale of earlier Indian painting, and not quite within the explosive radicalism of the new Indian art."* [34] *As to influences, he says, "I listen to no one. Yet everyone. My work is nothing more than work and more work. I experiment. I read. I live. These are my research materials."*

I was born in 1932 in Chinle, Arizona, on the Navajo reservation near Canyon de Chelly and lived there until I was ten. I spent much of my time with my grandmother, a sheepherder and farmer. Sitting under a tree, we'd milk the sheep and she'd show me how to make cheese. She had a splendid hogan built with rocks. Years later, the family tore it down and put up a shack made of boards. I guess they thought that was modern. My aunts live there today. They keep sheep for subsistence, but they can't make an adequate living as sheepherders. And they're afraid of being evicted from their land. [In accordance with the govern-ment's energy policy, Navajos are being removed from their land to make way for uranium and coal strip mines, coal gasification plants, and a nuclear waste disposal site.]

I remember Navajos with hundreds and hundreds of sheep, and old Navajos who had several wives because they were rich. They used the wool for rugs and blankets. But the government took away most of the sheep — took away their horses too — said they were overgrazing. Some of the wealthy Navajos were reduced to paupers overnight.

I remember the Chinle Valley when it was flooded every year. There were beautiful gardens every summer, fields of corn, beans, and melons. Today, they've dammed the water, and it's barren, very ugly. We lived comfortably in the fields and hogans. Today the people live in shacks; it's a ghetto. Young people today don't

R. C. Gorman, *Lady with Striped Blanket*. Oil pastel, 1979. Courtesy The Navajo Gallery.

know the way it used to look. I guess you can't go back to the way it was.

I return frequently to the reservation. I have family ties there. My mother and grandmother are dead, but I visit my Aunt Mary Tsosie, who helped raise me. She's as poor as a church mouse, but she's so generous with her heart, herself. You can't even give her a gift, because if someone comes along, she will give it away. She doesn't speak a word of English, but she says more by just being her beautiful, uncomplicated self than some people who have college degrees. And so I go back there. You can't turn your back on people who have loved you.

My father and I were very close when I was young, although he was in the service and we were rarely together. He took me on camping trips — just the two of us and a mangy gray cat. He cooked pork and beans and told uproarious stories that are with me to this day. I've just done a sculpture of my dad in bronze. As I worked on it, I remembered the times we were together.

As a boy, I attended boarding schools operated by missionaries. There was never enough to eat. We were not permitted to speak our language or to think for ourselves. Today, Indians on reservations are more independent and sophisticated, and they aren't so easily manipulated. I do think that, as a result, the church has

R. C. Gorman working on clay model for bronze sculpture of his father, artist Carl N. Gorman. Courtesy The Navajo Gallery.

R. C. Gorman, *Taos*. Lithograph, 1973. Courtesy The Navajo
Gallery.

had to grow, to begin to meet their needs. I'm a Christian in the
sense that I have all the fears the church instilled in me, but I
don't accept their view of the supernatural. I believe in being a
good person. However, I've been baptized in more than one
church, just to be on the safe side.

Some sects endow their religious leaders with an aura of mystery
and expect them to perform some sort of voodoo. For me, the
spiritual beings in Navajo sand paintings and ceremonies are not
god figures, and they're not perfect. I respect them as part of
nature.

I'm fascinated by the art and culture of the past. I've been to Egypt and other Arab countries. I love the sand dunes, but the guns are appalling. Why would anyone want to kill another human being?

I've been reading about the Jewish resistance to Roman rule in the first century A.D. The Romans thought they were invincible. They destroyed the Jewish temple and took over the holy city of Jerusalem. But a few hundred steadfast Jews would not give up their religion. They retreated to Herod's fortress, a fabulous condominium on the heights of Masada overlooking the Dead Sea. They held out there for years — men, women, and children. At the end, when the Roman legions finally stormed the fortress, they died fighting rather than submit. Such strength. I admire it, even though it was suicide.

We Navajos have our Masada. The Spaniards spent four centuries trying to conquer and convert the Southwest tribes, but they couldn't break the resistance of the Navajos. In the winter of 1805, Spanish soldiers drove a band of Navajo rebels from their camp within the steep rock walls of Canyon de Chelly and slaughtered them. A few old men and women and children remained hidden in a cave. The Spaniards found them and fired into the cave, killing them all. Since then, the place has been known as Canyon del Muerto, Canyon of the Dead. The bones are still there. You can hear them screaming at night. Those people died rather than give up their way of life.

I admire power, but I don't respect people who use or abuse others to get it. I wonder about this country's sense of justice. There are Nazis walking around today who in World War II were busy barbequing Jews. Some live in the United States. There's so little respect for human life. That really bothers me. I love everybody. It doesn't matter what their race or religion is — there's a human connection. I think people should be allowed to live their own lives according to their own values. I don't like to see anyone put down or oppressed for being different. I'm concerned about my people. I'm concerned about anyone who can't fight for himself.

R. C. Gorman, *The Gossips*. Silkscreen, 1978. Courtesy Suzanne
Brown Gallery.

Navajos love to give. They've given to the church, the government, the tourists, and they give to each other. They have little
left for themselves. If I didn't have people working for me who
depend on me, I'd give my paintings away. But that's not possible
anymore. You have to face reality — pay salaries, buy groceries.
People come to me constantly to support their causes and organizations. When scholarships are involved for young people, I try to
help.

I've been poor, but my people never starved. We always

had sheep and knew how to find wild plants. We always knew how to survive. Everyone should know what it is to be poor.

The women I paint work on the land. They need to be strong to survive. They have big hands, strong feet. Why are the faces not detailed? They're composites of many women I've known. Too many women think they're precious. I could never translate that into my life. I deal with the common woman who smells of the fields and maize. She lives and breathes. She's human.

Yesterday was my birthday. Friends had a surprise party for me. One delivered six bottles of champagne. I don't understand why people make such a fuss over me. I don't have a superego. I'm nobody. I'm just like everybody else. There are so many artists who are just doing their own thing and don't care if they're ever discovered. They're just being themselves. So am I.[35]

# Allan Houser,
## Apache sculptor

In 1862, Arizona Governor John Baylor issued the following instructions to the head of the Arizona Guards: "You will . . . use
all means to persuade the Apaches or any tribe to come in for the
purpose of making peace, and when you get them together kill all
the grown Indians and take the children prisoners and sell them to
defray the expense of killing the [adult] Indians." [36]

These orders were not carried out, but the dissident band of
Chiricahua Apaches, nomads and raiders at war with the U.S.
government for generations, was herded into Oklahoma Territory,
and on barren lands unsuitable for cultivation, they were ordered
to farm. The son of farmer Sam Haozous, Allan Houser was born
in 1914 in Apache, Oklahoma. (Because Anglos had difficulty pro-
nouncing the name Haozous, which means "pulling roots", it was
changed to Houser.) His parents expected him to be a cattleman,
but schooling under Dorothy Dunn at the Studio in Santa Fe
changed his destiny. He began painting murals in the flat, decorative style of the period. Then, with characteristic independence, he
moved on to depict Indian experiences realistically, even with a
touch of caricature.

Formal art training ended when Houser left the Santa Fe school,
but his work was already recognized. In 1937, he was the only Indian to be represented at New York City's National Exhibit of
American Art. Subsequently, he won commissions to paint murals

*for the Department of the Interior Building in Washington, D.C.,*
*the Southern Plains Indian Museum in Anadarko, Oklahoma, and*
*New York's World's Fair.*

*In search of new dimensions after World War II, Houser turned*
*to sculpture, working with wood, metal, clay, alabaster, and stones*
*found in the hills and mesas of New Mexico.  He received two*
*Guggenheim Fellowships, one for painting, one for sculpture.  As*
*director of the sculpture division of the Institute of American Indian*
*Arts from 1971 to 1975, Houser exerted a profound influence on*
*the work of young Indian sculptors.  His work is a part of the per-*
*manent collections of the country's leading museums.*

*Houser's sculpture reflects his interest in preserving the essence of*
*Indian culture.  Realistic elements contrast with abstraction, and*
*each piece has its own humanistic conception and majesty.*

I was born in Apache, Oklahoma.  My father and I worked a 160-
acre farm with horses.  He was a grandson of the Apache war chief
Mangus-Colorado and a distant relative of Geronimo.  My father
was too young to fight in the Apache wars with the U.S. government, but he spent his youth with people who had been on the
warpath.  After Geronimo's defeat, the tribe was almost destroyed.
The survivors lived under military rule in Fort Sill, Oklahoma,
virtually prisoners of war.  They were promised their own land,
but even today many of their claims have not been honored.

As I was growing up, my dad and others who had been through
the war with Geronimo told stories of those years and of the cap-
tivity.  My father knew Geronimo's war songs.  In the evenings we
would sit around a big wood stove.  He would sing, accompanying
himself with an Apache drum, and my mother would join in.
People would come from the Apache reservations in Arizona and
New Mexico to hear the songs that they had forgotten, that had
drifted down, like the stories, through the generations.

My dad knew the properties of many medicinal plants, and people came to him all the time — not only Apaches but Plains Indians too — for healing. I grew up very proud of my dad.

Farming was a struggle in those Depression years, and you had to work long hours to make a living. Occasionally, I would sit down and sketch something. Once, I used my pocket knife to carve a figure out of red cedar. It was of a man kneeling, hands on knees, as if singing a tribal song. But no one encouraged me to draw or carve, for I was needed on the farm, and they thought I should be working. I was discouraged, but I don't blame my family. No one made a living in art in those days.

I had other interests. I wanted to be a boxer, a baseball player. I didn't like being tied down in one place. But I realized I had to do something.

The Studio in Santa Fe was the only place in the United States where I could get a good education without a high-school di-

Allan Houser. Photo: Skip Holbrook, Institute of American Indian Art.

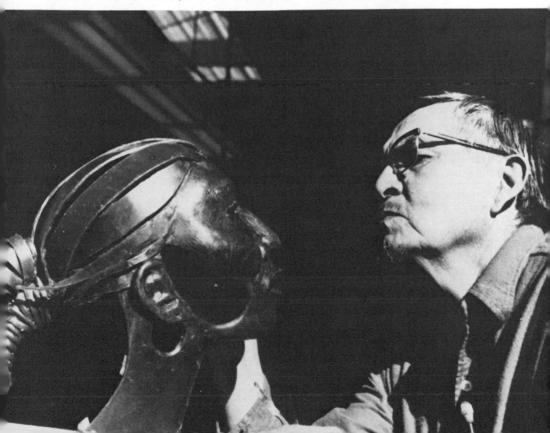

ploma. I left home and went there, determined to make something of the experience. The teacher at the Studio was trying to revive the old styles of Indian painting that had been practically lost — kiva murals, skin paintings, sand painting, drawings of the dances and ceremonies. It was exciting, but there was no chance to be creative. If you tried anything other than the traditional two-dimensional style, you were told you could catch the next bus for home. I knew the conditions at home. Besides, I was getting interested in art, so I stayed.

After finishing school, a friend and I opened up a studio in Santa Fe. We sold a few pieces for five dollars or ten dollars, but we were barely eating. Sometimes we had a cup of coffee between us. In fact, during most of the years I was painting, I was practically starving.

A chance came along to teach Navajos at the Intermountain School in Utah. The young people were there to learn different trades — auto mechanics, bricklaying — and this was a chance to broaden their horizons. I taught basic drawing techniques, textile painting, secco, and Italian fresco. My next job was as a teacher in a government school for Jicarilla Apache children. I taught mural painting to people in the community.

During World War II, I did construction work in Los Angeles. I was married and had four children to support. In my spare time, I went to the Otis Art Institute. I didn't attend classes, but I studied the sculpture there. I met a sculptor who encouraged me, told me what tools I needed, got me interested in stone. I had been groping. Suddenly, I saw myself involved in the creative process. I began experimenting and saw that anything was possible.

I've been sculpting for around thirty-five years. When I'm working, I get carried away. In my mind, I blow up a piece to twenty or thirty feet high. If I live long enough, I'd like to do monumental pieces in bronze and stone. You have to put yourself into something. When I design for steel, I think of steel. When I design for stone, I think of mass, volume, large smooth areas — not too much clutter, just what is essential. I think of strength.

Allan Houser, *Apache Spirit Dancer*. Bronze. Courtesy The Gallery Wall.

People ask me if there's a poetic vision. I don't think there really is. I express myself with my hands, trying to convey the sympathy between people. Often I just sit down with the clay and think of things I've seen. Then I try something new — elongate the figure, stylize it, play with new forms. I begin with reality,

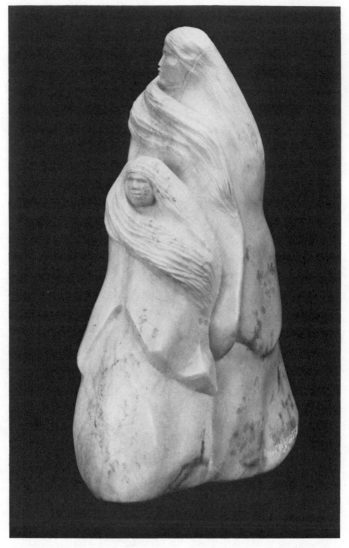

Allan Houser, *Together*.  Alabaster.  Courtesy The Gallery Wall.

but then go beyond reality.  I experiment with new concepts of design that challenge me.  I want to have impact on people.

My *Hunting Chant* is carved out of pink marble.  I'm trying to recapture the spirit of the nineteenth-century hunt.  The hunter prays to the Great Spirit — a chant or invocation for spirit power.

He closes his eyes, tries to visualize the location of the buffalo herd. He concentrates on the forward motion so intently, totally absorbed in the chase.

I visit the Apache reservations to stay in contact with the way things are and to remember who I am. Most of the old dances are still performed today, although some have lost their religious function. I did a piece in bronze called *Morning Song.* An older couple has danced the Apache Back and Forth, a social dance, most of the night. Now they sit and listen as the singers sing the morning song around the drums and the sun comes up. They're tired; they're in repose.

My son Robert Haozous is a sculptor. He works mostly in wood, marble, and alabaster. Although he shares my studio, he's never studied with me. He's developed his own, very distinctive style.

Allan Houser, *Morning Song.* Bronze. Courtesy The Gallery Wall.

Robert Haozous, *White Portrait Figure*.  Marble.  Photo: Herbert Lotz.

My work today is quite abstract.  I try to keep my thinking alive. I don't want to get stale.  I keep creating things that excite me.  I want something new to come out of everything I do.  I design, I play with new forms.  It comes more easily as you go along, because you're not afraid to attempt the things you visualize. Nothing will hold me back.  I'm thinking of steel, I'm thinking of concrete.  I'm reaching for the stars.[37]

# Grace Medicine Flower,
# Tewa potter

In the midst of New Mexico's lush Espanola valley, surrounded by the Jemez and Sangre de Cristo mountains, lies the pueblo of Santa Clara. One of its most celebrated residents is Grace Medicine Flower, member of a remarkable family of potters that traces its ancestry back to the Mimbres culture that flourished in the area in the twelfth century. Inspired by Mimbres pottery shards found at nearby excavation sites, Grace Medicine Flower's work suggests the fragile beauty and timelessness of her people. Her pottery is literally drawn from the earth, made from basic elements — earth, water, air, and fire. Working without a potter's wheel, using methods handed down from generation to generation, she meticulously shapes the fine, polished bowls that have won her wide-acclaim.

With her father, Camilio Tafoya, and her brother, Joseph Lonewolf, she has developed a two-color firing method done in one firing, which is said to be a refinement of a traditional process.

Using the sgraffito method, Grace Medicine Flower etches traditional designs and her own interpretation of traditional motifs onto the surface of the pottery. Eagle dancers, kachina dancers, plumed serpents abound in her work — mythic figures from Southwest Indian lore representing life-giving forces in the universe. Her designs give tangible form to the visions of a people for whom the past is an *ever present reality. She says, "The designs and visions come to me from the old ones. I must be true to them."*

I was born in 1938 in the old family home in Santa Clara pueblo. All our relatives came for my naming ceremony, and I was given six names. My mother called me Wopovi, which in the Tewa language means Medicine Flower. Her name was Yellow Flower. My father's name is Camilio Sunflower Tafoya.

I was raised in a close, loving family with aunts, uncles, and grandparents living nearby. On feast days we went to the plaza to watch the dances. When my father and brothers danced, I was very proud. Then relatives and friends gathered at our home — sometimes as many as fifty or a hundred people. We'd talk and laugh and eat the traditional foods prepared by the women in advance. The air was pungent with the odor of wild celery and cinnamon. There were huge, steaming pots of chile, and posole, a meat and vegetable dish. There was Indian bread freshly baked in the outdoor horno [beehive-shaped oven] and pies with thick, crisp crusts filled with prune, pumpkin, apples, and wild plum.

We lived in an adobe house with a few pieces of furniture, and a wood stove in the kitchen. There was no running water. My mother was always busy making pottery, so my brothers and I shared in the household chores, not because we had to but because we wanted to. They chopped wood, and I brought in the wood and water. When I was older, we had plumbing put in, and that made the chores easier.

We never had many toys. We drew pictures on the ground with sticks and made up our own games. I made the best mud pies in the pueblo.

My mother and father worked at pottery together. They made bowls and ollas [jars for carrying or storing water]. He sculpted horses out of clay and incised his designs onto the surface of the

Grace Medicine Flower.  Photo: Joe Becker, Jr.  Courtesy of the artist.

pottery. He was one of the first male potters in the pueblo. They sold their work on the portal in Santa Fe. That was our income; that's how we lived.

My father sometimes hunted in the mountains for deer. We ate the meat and dried what we did not eat, and my father used the skins to make moccasins for us. I was embarrassed to wear them, for the other children laughed at me, but now I think I should have been proud to wear them.

In earlier times, my father tells me, parents taught the children at home. Girls were expected to be potters, for the pots were needed as cooking utensils. Families would go to the Rio Grande for water, and the women would carry the water back in the jars they had made. My dad didn't think it was important for girls to attend school because he felt they'd get married and wouldn't need an education.

My mother encouraged me to learn as much as possible because one day, she said, things would be different for women. And now they are. My brothers and I walked about a mile to the Santa Clara Day School, a Bureau of Indian Affairs school for Indian children. I liked school. Sometimes a truck came and brought us eggs and potatoes. In the commissary, you could get shoes and stockings for the winter. Our teacher was non-Indian, but she lived in the pueblo and was a part of the community. In the afternoons, I went to her home to help her with paperwork, and she helped me with my homework. It was hard learning English as a second language. To this day I think in Tewa. Once you learn an Indian language, it's a part of you. I was taught by whites, but their world never took over completely. My Indian language and traditions always came first. Today, schools are offering courses in the tribal languages; that way, the heritage will be kept alive.

When I was young, I took part in the tribal dances, and I still do today. I love the excitement of getting ready for the dance and the colorful costumes that have not changed through the centuries. The women of our clan wear a white manta, a one-piece dress taken up at the right shoulder, with a woven belt. We do the Corn Dance and the Evergreen Dance to bring a plentiful harvest, and the Rainbow Dance to ask for rain. The Buffalo Dance used to be done to insure a successful hunt; now it's symbolic. My favorite is the Deer Dance. Young men and boys represent the deer that were once plentiful. At the sound of a gunshot, the "deer" run in every direction. If a girl or woman catches one, she must feed him feast foods, and he in turn brings her food.

It's important to dance the steps and sing the words of the songs carefully, for these are sacred ceremonies. The spirits of our ancestors who have gone before us to another world will see and hear and will assist us in whatever is needed by the tribe: the rain, the growth of crops, the good health of the people. Traditions are changing, but we still dance because it is our people's way.

My mother taught me how to work the clay. She said, "Here's a piece of clay. Make it beautiful." The Clay Lady, Mother told me, is in the next world; she's everybody's relative. She is the spirit of past generations that comes back in the clay. And so every day I pray to the Clay Lady before I work with the clay. I ask her to make it beautiful. I say whatever is in my heart.

The clay comes from the earth. Mother Earth gives us food, animals, plants. Everything exists because of her. We go to the hills near Santa Clara to get enough clay for a whole season. That's Indian land, and the clay is only for the pueblo. We put the clay in the sun to dry, soak it in water for about three days, then put it through a fine screen to get all the impurities out. I add a white powder to the clay to strengthen it, mixing it with my feet on a tarpaulin on the floor. When the clay has just the right consistency, I begin my pot, using the old coil method. I mold the coils by hand, then use gourds to smooth them. After the pot is formed and completely dry — that takes days — I sandpaper it and wet it down to remove the sandpaper lines. I cover the bowl with a red earth clay. This red slip comes from La Bajada Hill near Santa Fe. I hand-polish the bowl with stones my mother used to use — she left them to me. My mother was a wonderful potter. She died when I was eighteen. I always think her stones will help me.

Then it's time to incise designs onto the pot, freehand. This takes weeks or months. Your hand must be very steady, because nothing can be erased. I use knives and special tools my dad fashioned from nails. The designs I like best are the feather pattern — the feathers are from the eagle and mean strength; the kiva steps — that's a traditional design; and the pueblo dancers. Before I start designing, I ask the Clay Lady which design is best for a particular pot. I ask for help, and I do think she helps me.

The firing is done in the open on the ground. It has to be a really calm day, with no wind. We fire early in the morning or late in the evening. We put wood chips on the ground. Tin cans hold a steel grate, and a wire basket containing the pots is placed on the grate. The old way was to surround the fire with cow dung to hold the heat in, but now we use bark. You have to watch the fire carefully. If the wind blows and soot gets on the pot, it is ruined. If there's a small crack, your work is lost. Sometimes a pot you've worked on for months breaks. You can't be angry or discouraged. My dad will say, "The old ones, the ones that went before, are putting you through a test to see if you've put your whole self into a bowl or have done it just for commercial rea-

Pottery by Grace Medicine Flower. Photo: Joe Becker, Jr. Courtesy of the artist.

sons." If you fail, you say, "This is the way it was meant to be," and you go on working.

There are new methods now used in potterymaking, but I like to do it the way my family has done it for generations. I like carrying on the traditions.

My husband and I used to live in another town. I thought I'd go to work in the city. But after Mother died, we came here to be with Dad. He lives with us. Dad said, "Certain people are picked by the Clay Lady to work with the clay." Since that day, I have done pottery every day. My husband takes care of the house and is my manager. My father and I work at our kitchen table. Dad tells stories of the way it used to be. The day goes so fast. I love that man and respect him. He's seventy-six, and he still does beautiful work.

I'm happy with my life. I go to the city to shop, to meet people, and to attend the opera. But this is my home, and I wouldn't live anywhere else. People often come to our home to buy my work. I like to know that they will love my pottery and will care for it. They will admire the Clay Lady and give her a good home, for she really lives on in each piece of pottery.[38]

*Tewa Song*

*My home over there, my home over there,*
*My home over there, now I remember it!*
*And when I see that mountain far away*
*Why, then I weep . . .*

# Helen Hardin,
## Tewa painter

*The Tewa people, according to their lore, emerged from the underworld through a hole in Sip-ophe, a small lake in Colorado's sand dune country. Since the fourteenth century, they have lived in relative harmony in the pueblo of Santa Clara and other New Mexican pueblos, united by a complex belief system and ceremonial life. For the most part, their social and sacred institutions have survived despite the incursions of the Spanish, the missionaries, and the technology and economic pressures that came with the twentieth century.*

*Helen Hardin was born in 1943 and grew up in Santa Clara at a time when control was passing from a religious hierarchy to the town's younger, more progressive element. Like others of her generation educated in white schools, she refused to be defined or constrained by the roles predetermined for women by centuries of tradition in Santa Clara.*

*The daughter of Pueblo artist Pablita Velarde and Herbert O. Hardin, Helen Hardin painted from early childhood, winning her first art contest at the age of six. She worked hard to establish for herself an identity different from that of her mother, a traditional painter. After successful shows in Colombia and Guatemala, she entered exhibits in this country, winning six Grand Awards and two Best of Show awards, and is today one of the Southwest's leading artists.*

*A highly articulate individual with a variety of talents, Hardin has illustrated children's books and was the only woman artist to be featured in the PBS documentary, "American Indian Artists."*

*Unlike her mother, who with a metate (grinding stone used by Tewa women to grind corn) grinds natural materials to produce earth colors for her paintings, Hardin uses acrylics, inks, washes, and acrylic varnish in her work, which is as contemporary as her thinking.*

*Her Indian name is Tsa-sah-wee-eh, which means Little Standing Spruce.*

I've always had a clear sense of my Indian identity. I was born in Albuquerque in 1943 and spent my early years with my mother, Pablita Velarde, in the Santa Clara pueblo where she was born and grew up. My father, Herbert Hardin, was in the army during World War II. When he left the service, he continued his education, then took a job with the Albuquerque Police Department, and we moved there.

When my brother and I entered school, my mother, who had painted from childhood, returned to painting full-time. My dad was becoming more and more absorbed in his work. They developed separate lives and interests, and eventually the marriage fell apart. My father went to work in Washington, D.C., and we remained in Albuquerque.

I was an adolescent when my family broke up, and I experienced a sense of isolation. With father gone, and mother totally involved in her own work, there was little parental guidance.

My mother was dedicated to her art and painted continually. She went from a very traditional style in which she used caseins and temperas into the period where she developed her earth painting, using colored sand, rocks, dirt, and clay. She depicted scenes from everyday Pueblo life. Especially for women, Pueblo life was

Helen Hardin. Cradoc Bagshaw photo.

firmly rooted in tradition. A young woman was expected to make pottery just like her mother, to have babies, and to attend to her home and family. Everything that was expected of you had to happen. My mother had departed from this pattern by becoming a painter at a time when only men painted at Santa Clara. But in her style she remained a traditionalist.

Pablita has a very good sense of design and she incorporated the traditional ceremonies, those that could be seen publicly, into her paintings. [Persecuted by the Spanish conquerors for practicing their religion, Southwest tribes held many of their ceremonies secretly in the kivas or ceremonial chambers.] In the early forties, the people faithfully practiced their ceremonies in accordance with seasonal cycles. The songs and chants, the costumes and roles of tribal members had been handed down through the generations. After World War II the ceremonies were still held, as they are today, but had less impact on the people. Young Indian men returned from the service to find that there were GI benefits. They could get an education, they could get work in the cities. They didn't have to farm anymore. If you didn't farm, you didn't have to pray for rain in the spring. If you didn't harvest, you didn't have to do the harvest dance in the fall. They had pickup trucks, access to cities, better food, but also more refined food. Because of a taste for sweets and their lack of education as to proper nutrition, the people became susceptible to obesity, tooth decay, and various diseases. Liquor was more available. Heart attacks became more common. Most of the people no longer believed that the old healing ceremonies had the power to cure disease. And yet today, whenever they are fed up with the Public Health doctors, they may call in a medicine man to perform a healing ceremony, although it is often too late.

I felt excluded from the traditional Pueblo world that my mother was a part of. I watched her paint, and I painted just like her. And people would come along and say, "Oh Helen, you're painting just like your mommy." And they patted me on the head because I was such a nice little girl. But I hated it.

My mother didn't teach me. She let me do what I wanted to do as long as I painted in the traditional way. I copied designs from books and from other artists. I painted dances and ceremonies that Mother remembered, but that I had never seen. When I was around eighteen, I began to experiment. I became involved with Pueblo mythology, started painting circles and triangles, and incorporated Indian designs into my paintings. Some of these abstract concepts crept into my mother's work, but still people would say, "Oh, Helen is painting just like Pablita." No one gave me credit for innovating.

Helen Hardin, *Medicine Talk*. Acrylic. James T. Bialac Collection, Phoenix, Arizona. Cradoc Bagshaw photo.

I went to the University of New Mexico and studied art history and anthropology, but I became bored with the structure and discipline. I attended the Special School for Indian Arts at the University of Arizona. At nineteen I held my first one-woman show. Not long after that, I was married.

A few years later, I awoke to the fact that I was twenty-four years old, I was locked into an unhappy marriage, and I was not painting. I didn't know who I was or what I was. In search of personal freedom, I took Margarete, my three-year-old daughter, and left the country.

We went to my father's home in Bogota, Colombia, where he was then chief of public safety with AID. He had a very large house with servants. It was my first experience with affluence, with security, and with no one making demands on me. I felt free for the first time in years, and I began painting again.

I began with traditional themes, but the designs and compositions came freely from my imagination. People encouraged me.

Helen Hardin, *Robed Images*. Acrylic. Courtesy Fenn Gallery, Santa Fe, New Mexico. Cradoc Bagshaw photo.

No one had heard of my mother, no one patted me on the head and bought my paintings because I was Pablita's daughter. I had a one-woman show in Bogota. People were overwhelmed, and they bought paintings because they saw that my work was unique.

I returned to New Mexico with something I had never possessed before — self-confidence. I rented an inexpensive apartment, bought a small car, and Margarete and I started a new life. I set goals for my work and for my own life. I worked with intense discipline, painting long hours every day in preparation for shows, and we survived those first difficult years. Gradually, I began attracting the attention of the art world.

That dedication to art remains a part of my life. I return often for inspiration to the places I visited as a child: the Puyé Cliffs, the great canyons, and the abandoned pueblos. The traditional symbols appear in my work: the mythical beings found in rock art, kachina dancers, the sun, the eagle — guardian of the sky — but I adapt and rearrange the designs, based on my own intuitive sense. I work with silhouettes, stylization of faces and figures, geometric patterns inspired by the designs on the pottery of the ancients, and abstract forms. I experiment with layout, with the application of color, with textures, with variations on a motif.

Traditional Indian art uses the symbols of a particular culture to depict a scene, tell a story. As a contemporary artist, I'm concerned with evoking a feeling, conveying an impression. I translate the images of Indian cultures into new visual metaphors that speak to all people.

I think I have always been spiritual in my art, not in a structured Pueblo religious sense, but in the sense of being alive and human. I express that sense of affirmation in my work. I'm happy now as a human being. I'm very competitive. I'm a very strong person. I will not be stepped on, ignored, or pushed aside without protest. Women have not been recognized for so long. Now they're showing the world that they can write music and fly planes, dig ditches, build buildings, and paint paintings as well as any man.

My imagination is the soul of my work. Every painting sings its own song. It reflects the mood I'm in today, or the season. I love my Indian heritage, and I draw on it. I paint my spiritual response to the Indian experience. I use tradition as a springboard and go diving into my paints.[39]

*From the Navajo Mountain Chant*

*The voice that beautifies the land!*
*The voice above,*
*The voice of the thunder*
*Within the dark cloud*
*Again and again it sounds,*
*The voice that beautifies the land.* [40]

# Part 2
# The Performing Arts

*We Indians can dance all the colors of the
rainbow . . . . I sing the songs of both our
summer and our winter.*

*Buffy Sainte-Marie*

Anthropologists and ethnologists have amassed a wealth of factual data about tribal ceremonies. But it is the Native American, who has received the tribal language as a birthright, to whom we must look for a faithful rendering of the spirit of these gatherings.

George Clutesi, poet of the Nootka on the Northwest Coast, interweaves narrative and song in his extended prose poem "Potlatch." It is an attempt to capture the mood and theatricalism of the potlatch ceremony as it is practiced in one form or another by Northwest Coast tribes. In Clutesi's poetic account, the drama takes place in an improvised theater:

> The right side — the side away from the river — of the lodge . . . had been quietly vacated and half the entire length of the . . . low platform that ran below and along the raised living quarters had been removed and placed on top of the other half . . . to create a screen . . .
>
> Pooffff!
>
> The silence was broken by the distinct sound of a whale blowing in the distance.
>
> Pooffff! There it was again; clearly and distinctly the sound drifted into the lodge from the direction of the open doors.

Smoke spirals from the fire, there is the roll of a rattle, a voice intones a song to Ee-toop, the great whale, and from behind the

screen the prow of a whaling canoe moves into view, followed by a
crew of eight men who hold their paddles deep in the imagined
waters.

> Pooffff!
> Slowly, majestically Ee-toop rose from behind the
> screen, the dark red of its blood directly below the dorsal
> fin rolling and rippling ever so slightly from the draft
> created in the low passageway behind the screen.[41]

Such an event, so graphically depicted by Clutesi, represents
weeks, even months, of activity, during which the community has
pooled its creative energies. Canoemakers, songmakers, in-
strumentalists, dancers, actors, directors, makers of costumes,
masks, and scenic effects work in secrecy, taking care that all is
done promptly and "with the utmost gravity." The result of their
efforts is an affirmation of tribal solidarity.

Few Indian ceremonials are more theatrical than the forty-nine-
day ritual of the Zuni Indians, the Shalako. It re-enacts the Zuni
emergence and migration, as well as the return of the dead.
Huge, masked figures impersonate the Shalako, or messengers of
the deities:

> At noon, on this forty-ninth day, the Shalako leave.
> Gliding past house tops thronged with people, they
> gather at the river. In the bright, warm sunlight they
> loom bigger, brighter, stranger than at night. Escorted
> by flutists and singers anointed with pinches of meal,
> they cross the causeway and glide swiftly away from rev-
> erent Zuni. Glide back to their source, disappearing as
> suddenly as they came. But to come again and mingle
> with their people . . .[42]

An Eskimo shaman is likely to indulge in displays of histrionics
as he or she stages music and dance events, the central feature of
which is the use of "magic words." The shaman develops a form
of secret language in which all things referred to are disguised.
The formulas, according to Jerome Rothenberg, must be con-

tinually changed or revitalized, or they will lose their power.[43]
The shaman is a charismatic figure.

The contemporary dancer or choreographer, actor or playright, instrumentalist or composer draws from this storehouse of tribal traditions, but must exercise great care in the presentation of sacred material, for such exposure is still considered sacrilegious by some tribal people.

Rosalie Jones.  Courtesy National Indian Education Association.

In the performing arts, as in the visual arts, there is a continual process of change and adaptation. Today's performer often employs the contemporary idiom, even though the context may be traditional. Blackfeet dancer Rosalie Jones, for example, interprets the songs and legends of many tribes in individualistic dance forms.

The 1970s saw the genesis of all-Indian theater companies, beginning with the formation of the Native American Theatre Ensemble in New York City by Hanay Geiogamah, a Kiowa-Delaware Indian, under the auspices of La Mama Experimental Theatre. Other groups came into being: The Navajo Trucking Company; Echo Hawk, a Chicago-based company; and Seattle's Red Earth Performing Arts Company.

The 1970s also saw Indian filmmakers come to the fore and Indian actors cast in Indian roles that had some semblance of reality. Chief Dan George, a hereditary chief of the Squamish Indians of Vancouver and a Tribal Council president, distinguished himself in the role of Old Lodge Skins in the film *Little Big Man*. Will Sampson, a Creek Indian from Oklahoma, was doing everything "from painting pictures to bustin' bulls" before winning acclaim in the role of Chief Bromden in the film *One Flew Over the Cuckoo's Nest*.

Television appearances have brought Oneida comedian Charlie Hill national attention, and have paved the way for a film career. Hill quips:

> I went to Hollywood because I heard they were using Indians to play human beings . . . In Hollywood they ask me how mean I can look, will I shave my chest for a part, or can I ride a horse. They never ask me if I can act."[44]

Indian folk-singer Buffy Sainte-Marie, a Canadian Cree, has a wide following. She has moved away from the angry protest songs of a decade ago, and says now that she wants Indians "to come and hear triumphant music that underlines the joy, beauty and dignity of being Indian."[45]

Less celebrated, but no less dedicated is Sioux balladeer Floyd Westerman who travels Indian land, singing and conveying his message that "only by being true to Indian values will this society avert destruction." Westerman satirizes anthropologists in a song written in collaboration with Jimmy Curtiss and Vine Deloria, Jr.:

> . . . And the anthros keep on digging our ceremonial
>     site,
> As if their education had given them the right.
> But the more they keep on digging the less they really
>     see,
> 'Cause they got no respect for you and for me . . . [46]

*Songs are thoughts, sung out with the breath*
*when people are moved by great forces and ordinary*
*speech no longer suffices . . .*

*It is just as necessary for me to sing as it is to*
*breathe. I will sing this song, a song that is strong.* [47]
                    *Orpingalik, Netsilik Eskimo*

# Louis Ballard,
## Quapaw/Cherokee composer

"Music is as old as the world. We came onto this earth singing," Louis Ballard tells students at the many workshops in tribal and contemporary music he conducts nationwide.

Ballard has won international recognition as a composer of symphonic and chamber music, art songs for choral groups, percussion and piano pieces, and film scores. Symphonic pieces include Why the Duck Has a Short Tail, an Indian musical legend for orchestra, and Portrait of Will Rogers, a multimedia piece honoring a great Indian American. His ballet scores include Koshare, commissioned by the Harkness Ballet, and The Four Moons, commissioned by the National Endowment for the Arts and the state of Oklahoma.

An innovator, Ballard seeks not to imitate but to capture the essence of Indian music and to blend it with Western musical traditions. His woodwind quintet Ritmo Indio draws on nature's rhythms, which are the basis for the chants and dances of tribal music. Incident at Wounded Knee was commissioned by Dennis Russell Davies and the Saint Paul Chamber Orchestra and premiered in 1974. It was inspired by the U.S. Army's massacre of Indians at Wounded Knee, South Dakota, in 1890, and the Indians' dramatic return to the town in 1973.

Ballard has served as chairman of both the Music and the Performing Arts departments at the Institute of American Indian Arts. In 1977, he wrote the narration and music for the first National

*Indian Honor Band concert and pageant, based on the lives of Indian historical figures and presented in the nation's capital by Indian students representing eighty tribes. Young people painted murals for the performance and danced tribal dances. A 150-piece all-Indian marching band played the National Anthem, and students mimed it in Indian sign language in this tribute to their heritage.*

*The holder of five National Indian Achievement Awards and the annual EdPRESS Award for Educational Journalism, Ballard has had impact on the lives of young people. "They are creating new songs," he says. "There are songmakers by the hundreds among the Indians on reservations — an indication that our musical heritage is very much alive."*

My Indian name is Hunka-Nozhe, which means Grand Eagle. According to custom, the name was given to me by an elder of my mother's tribe, the Quapaws.

Our original tribal name is Ogáxpa, but the English settlers could not transcribe it properly, and reduced it to Quapaw. Our people originally lived in Arkansas, and we were known as the "Downriver People." There were twelve to fifteen thousand Quapaws living in the territory when de Soto explored it in 1541.

In 1830, under pressure from white officials and settlers, the Quapaw leaders signed a treaty at Dancing Rabbit Creek ceding their lands to the U.S. government. They received in exchange only empty promises. The Quapaws became wanderers, homeless for many decades. This was our Trail of Tears. [A reference to the Cherokee removal of 1838. Known as the Trail of Tears, the forced march to Oklahoma left 60 per cent of the Cherokee Nation dead.] Ultimately, the people settled around Spring River in northeastern Oklahoma, where they still live today.

After the dispersal, most of the traditional culture eroded. By

Louis Ballard with American Indian Creative Percussion Ensemble, performing at National Folk Festival, Wolf Trap Farm Park, 1973. Photo: William E. Dunning. Courtesy of New Southwest Music Publications, Santa Fe, New Mexico.

the 1930s, only fifteen to twenty people spoke the tribal language, a form of Lakotah, fluently. Today, no one does. Intermarriage further diluted tribal influences. Today, there are only three or four Quapaw full-bloods alive.

On my father's side I am Cherokee. I was born in Devil's Promenade, Oklahoma. When I was six, I was sent fifty miles from the reservation to attend a government-operated boarding school. This was in reality a brainwashing center for young Indians. There I was subjected to a reform-school "education." We were punished severely if we spoke Indian languages or danced tribal dances. I lived in a barracks with 300 other boys. I had to make my bed well enough to bounce a quarter on it. I remember crying my eyes out because I couldn't do it. Whenever one of us had a cold, we were lined up in a row and forced to take cough syrup — all from the same spoon. I saw my "gulag archipelago" in the first grade.

I cried my way out of there. My parents were divorced and my stepfather's job took my mother away from the reservation, but she brought me to my grandmother's house. Grandmother had land allotted to her under the Dawes Commission. [Tribal lands were carved up under the Allotment Act of 1887, supervised by the Dawes Commission, with small plots going to Indians for farming, the rest to whites seeking an end to reservations. As allotted lands were divided among a family's heirs, individual holdings dwindled almost to nothing. So Indians were divested of land, livelihood, and pride.] There, my brother and I were protected from the pressures and taboos of the dominant society. We attended a reservation school. We played football, baseball, threw rocks into the water, swam across the river with our dog, and felt free.

Periodically, we were sent to live with Mother in Wyandot, Michigan. We were often ostracized because we were Indian. The teacher would ask us to draw tom-toms and tomahawks, while others drew trees and puppies. After school, the white students often chased us and threw rocks.

Returning to the reservation, we were transferred to the Baptist Mission School. I suspect Grandmother had turned Baptist to get along with the whites who dominated the reservation. They said that to survive one had to embrace Jesus Christ. But I sensed that there was another force. My great-grandfather had been a medicine man in the Native American Church, and that religion was still very much alive among Indians.

Although my people were farmers, there was music in our home. My mother had learned to play the piano at the Mission School, and she taught us to play the old songs — the Quapaw Face Dance, the Turkey Dance. She composed songs.

Grandmother came into a windfall. Lead and zinc were discovered beneath Quapaw lands, and white entrepreneurs sought to obtain the land through purchase, leasing, or, when all else failed, intermarriage with Indians. Grandmother retained her land, and with her lease payments she bought a piano. So began the Saturday rituals that were to last for years: piano lessons, voice lessons — even tap dancing. The piano became my surrogate mother and father. It was reliable; it was always there.

I continued to live in two worlds. The reservation was a comfortable place, with communal events, powwows, and feasts in the summer. But whenever I was with my parents, I was confused, for they had not resolved the riddle of their existence in two societies. I knew that I had to find my way in both worlds.

In high school, I played football, studied art, and was encouraged to perform on the piano. In the tenth grade, I played Edward MacDowell's *Concert Etudes* at the University of Oklahoma. My family was proud of me, but there were very few pressures to succeed. The impetus came from inside me.

In college, I painted in the traditional style of Indian art, but found that through music I could better express my vision of the cosmos. In my musical studies at the University of Oklahoma I was confronted with the clichés of Western composers who in the 1920s wrote pseudoethnic Indian music based on their impressions of tribal songs. But they didn't know our culture. I was determined to bridge that cultural gap, to develop a distinctly Indian voice.

I was, and still am, a traditionalist, closely identified with what is left of Indian culture. For one of my earliest exercises in composition, I arranged a Ponca Indian round in the style of Chopin and Rachmaninoff. But this was just another pseudoethnic music form. The concept of synthesizing Western and non-Western music, of bringing Indian music into the mainstream of America's consciousness, fascinated me. I continued to incorporate tribal song and dance in my work.

I have always sought direction, and some great teachers helped me to define my musical voice. I studied with Dr. Bela Rizsa, a Hungarian composer, and with Darius Milhaud at the Aspen Music Festival in Colorado. There I met my wife, Ruth Doré Ballard, a concert pianist, who encouraged me and performed my compositions. I commuted to Hollywood to study with the great

Italian-American composer Mario Castelnuovo-Tedesco. That was truly a pilgrimage.

Although I was trained in the modern idiom, tribal song remains the inspiration for much of my music. I am proud of the fact that I am an award-winning tribal singer and dancer. I belong to the War Dance Society of the Quapaw tribe, and when I return home I participate in the festivals. The War Dance is the last vestige of a once flourishing and vibrant dance tradition. We still try to recapture the spirit of victory. It is as meaningful as the Scottish Sword Dance, the Kabuki rituals, and the songs of the troubadors.

When I was music director at the Institute of American Indian Arts in 1962–1968, I developed a modern choral approach, using American Indian songs from as many as fifty different tribes. Students learned to chant in the authentic style of the tribal musician, to enunciate sounds and vocables. They acquired some grasp of the cultural context of Indian vocal music. It differs from jazz and religious music, and usually does not adhere to the European tempered scale. A Hopi song differs from a Dakotah song, just as gypsy music differs from German *lieder*. Singing tribal songs gives young people self-esteem and a sense of history. Chief Luther Standing Bear of the Sioux wrote that the blood of our ancestors is in the soil of this land. We have songs about mountains, trees, rivers, and deserts because we revere them and will not defile them.

In my workshops for Indian and non-Indian students, I may play an Indian love song on the courting flute — that's a traditional instrument — and then many variations on a theme. I talk about the role the flute played in tribal courting rituals. The study of Indian music gives young people an opportunity to identify with their own indigenous music. They come to appreciate its intrinsic beauties, subtleties, and complexities.

In my composition for woodwind quintet *Ritmo Indio*, the flute takes the place of the oboe in the second movement. *Devil's Promenade*, an orchestral work, utilizes the water drum, war drum, Seneca cow-horn rattle, seashell rattles, tom-tom, and Dakotah drum, as well as the celeste, glockenspiel, triangles, and violins. *Cacega Ayuwipi*, a percussion piece, utilizes over forty Indian instruments and standard percussion.

Indian lore provides the inspiration for many of my compositions. The ballet *Koshare* deals with the Hopi creation story and the evolution of the people. Another ballet, *The Four Moons*, featured four internationally acclaimed Amerindian ballerinas: Maria Tallchief (Osage), Yvonne Choteau (Cherokee), Rosella Hightower (Choctaw), and Moscelyne Larkin (Shawnee), re-creating the spirits of four tribes that have returned to earth. I designed the costumes and sets for this work.

*Incident at Wounded Knee*, for chamber orchestra, is a response to the massacre of the Oglala Sioux in 1890 at Wounded Knee, South Dakota, and the Indians' symbolic occupation of the town in 1973. A series of musical episodes depict the emotional procession toward the town, the state of souls in torment, and the violent conflict. The work culminates in musical and dance forms affirming the essential spirituality of Native American people. *Incident* is not a political work, but it drew a strong reaction from oppressed peoples when it was played in Poland and Czechoslovakia, as well as in the cities of Western Europe. The fact that I was taking a bow onstage with a white American orchestra and conductor did more than words can to show that we live in a free country.

My hope is to have Indian music evaluated on its own terms for its coherence as well as its intrinsic musical values. Only in this way will America have a music tradition truly its own.

South American composers Carlos Chavez, Ginastera, Revueltas, and Villa-Lobos — all of part-Indian descent — have had impact on contemporary music. They integrate their Indian heritage with the techniques of Western music as I have tried to do. But there are dynamic voices still on the outside looking in: the black African, and the Indonesian, East Indian, and other Orientals, as well as the Native American. These will come to the foreground in the twenty-first century. I am pleased to have played a part in this great new movement in music and cultural history.[48]

## A New Roundhouse, Northern California


. . . The gray smoke curls upward

. . . and the faces in the circle
of the roundhouse
are silent carvings
fashioned by fire.

The pit drum pulses
earth her heart beat
as shadows quiver and face
themselves upon the rounded wall.

A singer sends forth a plea
and his voice becomes the dancers' feet,
then I see the old one smile
as if the puffs of dust
were reliving all her seasons.

And rattlesnake and dry, wind-blown leaves
are in the voice of elderberry clapper,
and every bird or other
gentle sound that ever was
is retold by the dancers' whistles.

And the sounds and vision are one
with smoke and sky and dreaming
and night warmth sighs the grasses
and the oaks downslope whisper
their content that the people
are returned.

*In quiet wonder at this feast*
*I trail my thoughts in dust*
*unwinding recorded history*
*like leaves plucked by wind.*

Peter Blue Cloud, Mohawk

# Cecilia White,
# Tlingit dancer

The Tlingit Indians lived on coastal islands in the vicinity of Sitka, Alaska. Their social and religious life centered on the sea creatures and fur-bearing animals on which their lives depended. Ceremonies were held to ensure the continuance of the salmon, thought to be immortal. Shamans conducted rituals transferring powers from animals — particularly the land otter — to humans.

Like other Northwest Coast Indians, the Tlingit decorated their totem poles with crests that traced their descent from a supernatural animal such as the Raven, Eagle, or Bear. Chiefs and others of high lineage staged potlatches, or village celebrations, during which they displayed their crests and performed their special songs and dances, all evidence of high status and privilege.

Cecilia White is a member of a family that inherited chiefdom and the responsibilities that go with it. She grew up in Saxman, an Indian town established by missionaries in Southeast Alaska. Her ancestors were among the village's earliest settlers, having migrated there in the 1890s from Cape Fox Village. From their abandoned Tlingit village they brought the totem poles that once had marked their relatives' graves and the songs, dances, and ceremonies of their ancestors.

I am a Tlingit Indian. I was born in the village of Saxman, Alaska, in 1931. I was born at home, not in a hospital, with a midwife attending. My grandmother gave me the name Hah shee. My father was a fisherman. My mother was a very beautiful woman. They had thirteen children.

From my mother's side of the family I inherited the Raven Clan. [The Tlingit village was organized around clans or family groups. Clan membership involved rights and privileges that passed from a mother to her children and from a father to his sister's children.] I was raised by my grandmother. Her brother was one of the last traditional chiefs — the old form of government, with a strong council and chief, was passing. My grandmother was true to her Indian ways. She helped those who migrated to the village adjust to the new life. From her I learned respect for older people and for all life: the fowl, the birds, the fish in the sea, even the air we breathe. If you went out in a fishing boat, you were not fearful, for you respected the wind. You kept your mind straight and strong. *"Ka-too-woo,"* we say in Tlingit, speaking of the importance of one's frame of mind, the power of feelings.

Living so close to animals, we were taught that any form of life can overtake your mind. I remember hearing stories of a man who was taken by a female bear to live in her cave. It was understood that if a man was isolated, removed from humans, he might assume the animal's sense of smell and hearing and its eating habits. The people didn't question this; they accepted it.

A sense of the sacredness of a woman's responsibilities to her home and family was instilled in me from early childhood. I learned to tan hides, to make moccasins, to weave baskets out of cedar bark, and to sew raven and bear figures on blankets and clothing. I learned to cook the traditional foods. In the summer, we camped in tents or cedar-bark cabins and gathered berries, seaweed, and clams. The men brought in abalone and salmon, seal meat and deer meat, which we smoked or preserved in fish oils for the winter.

I married a man from another village clan, the Eagles, who had also been brought up in the traditional way. [Cecilia was not permitted to marry within her clan. Thus the Tlingit prevented the marriage of blood relatives.] Before hunting or fishing, he prepared his equipment very carefully himself. He had to be clean in body and mind, for fishing and hunting were sacred functions. When he went into the woods, he spoke to the wolves in the

Cecilia White. Photo: Kathryn Oneita.

Tlingit language, asking for safe passage. He'd say: "This is your territory. If it's within your will, let me pass through."

We had six children. In the early years, my husband was able to support the family as a fisherman. But as the children grew older, their needs increased. The commercial fishermen placed traps in the water, which reduced the supply of salmon, and it became more difficult for my husband to make a living.

There were many pressures on our people to give up our old way of life. The missionaries and public-school teachers taught that our religion was primitive, based on superstition. Many Indians left the village to find jobs, losing contact with their families and with tribal customs. Intermarriage further weakened tribal identity.

About thirty years ago, the elders began to counter these outside influences by teaching the younger generation about the Indian way of life. Many were the nights that we sang and danced and learned the legends of our totem animals. A special dance group was formed to provide singing and dancing lessons for the children. My family became involved in this group.

We moved to Seattle in 1969 to obtain better schooling for our children and a secure income. We formed a dance group based on the teachings of the elders in our village. My husband and I coordinate the programs, which are presented mostly in schools. We both dance, and he plays the handmade raw-skin drum. Our daughters and their husbands enact various roles in the ceremonies, wearing costumes that we make ourselves in accordance with the customs of our clan. Our clan wears a heavy blanket, or long shirt, of red and black felt decorated with abalone shells, and moccasins made of sealskins, deer hide, or rabbit fur. Masks and headdresses are usually carved from red cedar and may be decorated with fur.

Our dances follow the traditional pattern of the potlatch. The potlatch of the Tlingit is usually given to honor a guest or a newborn child, or to dedicate a longhouse or totem pole. The host chief begins the dancing. He wears moccasins, beaded shirt, and button blanket, and ermine fur streams down the back of his head.

The Cape Fox Dancers. Photo: Kathryn Oneita.

Women of the Beaver Clan perform the Beaver Dance, which illustrates our close relationship with animals. Then a boy does the Bow and Arrow Dance while a narrator tells the story of the boy who brought food to a starving village. A Memorial Dance pays tribute to lost loved ones. Other legends may be acted out. Finally, in full clan regalia, the whole group joins in the Potlatch Dance. We close with a song:

> *O Great Spirit*
> *Whose voice I hear in the winds,*
> *And whose breath gives life to all the world,*
> *Hear me:*
>
> *I am small and weak,*
> *I need your strength and wisdom.*

*Let me walk in beauty*
*And let my eyes ever behold*
*The red and purple sunset . . .*


When our children were young, my husband and I kept them
with us as much as possible.  They didn't sit in front of a TV set
for hours.  We taught them all they were able to absorb.  Now
they are teaching their children, who in turn will carry on the
traditions of the Tlingit people.[49]

# John Kauffman,
# Nez Perce actor and director

The landscape of the Northwest Coast provides an endless source of inspiration for the native storyteller. Every rock, river, or mountain peak has a history: "Before people were on the earth, the Chief of the Sky Spirits grew tired of his home in the Above World, because it was always cold up there. So he made a hole in the sky by turning a stone round and round. Through this hole he pushed snow and ice until he made a great mound that reached from the earth almost to the sky. Later, people named it Mount Shasta . . ." [50]

Properly speaking, these tribal tales should not be classified as myth or fantasy, for to many of the Indian elders they are real and full of meaning. Stories of Thunderbird devouring whales, and of the Changer transforming young girls into stars are inherently dramatic and provide the basis for Indian theater.

John Kauffman is a graduate of the University of Washington's Professional Actor's Training Program. He has acted in productions staged by the Seattle Repertory Theater, the Empty Space Theatre, and A Contemporary Theatre, all in Seattle; by the Citadel Theater in Edmonton; and by the Center Theater Group in Los Angeles. He has appeared on television as guest star in the series "McCloud," and in the role of a dissident Nez Perce warrior in the story of Chief Joseph's life, "I Will Fight No More Forever."

Kauffman has directed War Play at Seattle's Ethnic Cultural

*Center and* The Fantastics *at* A Contemporary Theatre. *His one-man production of* The Indian Experience, *a docudrama that he wrote with Wayne Johnson, is an interpretation of Indian history, culture, and contemporary issues from a multitribal perspective, through the medium of poetry, speeches, song, and dance.*

━━━━━

When I was growing up, I used to spend hours listening to my grandmother tell stories about the lives of Indian leaders. My favorite was Chief Joseph, the Nez Perce leader who outwitted the U.S. Army. She told about how lakes and mountains were formed. There were tales about Indian ghosts. I loved hearing the adventures of Raven and the trickster Coyote. I was a dreamer, and these stories stirred my imagination.

I was born in 1947 near the Nez Perce Reservation in Idaho. My mother is full-blooded Nez Perce, my father is German. My grandparents lived on the reservation, and we visited them often.

We attended religious ceremonies on the reservation. One is called Talmaks. It is held in an enormous tent, with the people living in tipis for two weeks. The Nez Perce language is used, but basically it's a Christian service. Many people had lost contact with the language, and the old songs and ceremonies were dying out. But the people felt a great sense of loss and began to revive them. I remember the powwows we went to — I still go to them when I return home. I love the dance competitions, the drumming, and the singing. At these events, the spirit of our people is very much alive.

I was sometimes ribbed by Indians for being half-white, but my Indian identity was always clear in my mind. The first time I encountered hostility toward Indians was in elementary school: We saw a film about the "massacre" of U.S. forces by "savage Indians." I realized they were talking about my people, and that really hurt. Then in junior high school, one of my teachers spoke

John Kauffman. Photo: Jerry W. Smith.

of "the savage and cruel Nez Perce." When I protested that this was a distortion of history, he changed the subject. I buried myself in books about Indian history and contemporary affairs and developed strong convictions about the economic plight of Indians, reservation government, and fishing rights. I wondered how I could make a contribution.

My parents had hoped that I would go to law school, but even in high school, I was hooked on theater. I played the comic lead in the high school play — the dumb guy. Playing a dumb guy is difficult, because he thinks he's smart. Your timing has to be just as fast as for any other role, but the choices your character makes are all the wrong ones. If you play a villain, you must steep yourself in evil. Every actor has to believe that he or she is crucial to the play. This makes the play come alive. If you watch artists like Laurence Olivier and Glenda Jackson, your attention is riveted to center stage, but they always know when to lessen their presence, to shift the focus to their fellow actor. You only find prima donnas in mediocre houses or amateur theater. If you treat your craft as a profession, you're not concerned with feeding your ego. Presenting a play is a group process.

The sensation of acting is a real high, demanding your very best. You must maintain a high level of honesty for a long period of time in an unreal situation. You're performing before an audience. The walls of the set and all the props are artificial; people are making noise behind the set, and yet you must be totally absorbed in the character you've created. You have an interior monologue going on all the time. You go through all the stages of development that your character goes through: the conflicts, mood changes, the highs and lows. You have to find all these emotions within yourself. Every character is a variation of yourself. You must commit yourself emotionally.

Since the age of thirteen, I've tried to understand the world of my emotions — who I am, why I do what I do. That's a natural part of growing up if you're a thinking person, but it's never easy. There's agony involved in being creative.

When I direct a play, my perspective shifts. I have to think in terms of plot development, the hills and valleys of a scene, what's most significant. In a film, the camera will zero in on what it wants the audience to see. On stage, the director determines the focus. We begin rehearsals with game playing to loosen the actors up. One involves throwing an imaginary ball back and forth. When you have the ball, the focus is on you; everyone waits to see where it goes next. You must concentrate and direct all your energy toward a goal. As they build characters, the actors must learn style. Each type of theater, whether it's Ibsen, Pinter, Shakespeare, or Native American theater, has its own style. The emotional process is the same for the actor, who must grasp the feeling from within, then extend it so that it reaches the audience. The style varies from play to play. In Native American theater, the style is often naturalistic, often broad, but it must be honest.

I had intensive training in theater at the University of Washington, on a scholarship provided by my tribe. I wanted to use Indian theater to put across Indian culture and values. That was the sixties. Others were picketing on campus and in the streets. Through militancy, they advocated fair treatment for minorities. On stage, in the glare of the footlights, I would have my say.

I put together a show examining the Native American experience through theater, music, and dance. We took it to schools all over the state of Washington — it was a hit — then to Broadway, and back to Seattle. With a man called Donald Matt, I was asked to start an all-Indian theater in Seattle under the auspices of the United Indians of All Tribes Foundation. That was the beginning of the Red Earth Performing Arts Company — five people, no money. We all had other jobs so we could eat. Eventually I got a CETA grant. We did a review called *Coyote Speaks*. The King County Arts Commission took it on tour, and we received a grant from the National Endowment for the Arts. Now we could pay salaries, royalties for plays, and theater rental fees, and buy costumes. Actors began coming to Seattle. Doors kept opening, and

The Red Earth Performing Arts Company. Photo: Jerry W. Smith.

we kept growing. The financial support really made the difference.

The most important thing about ethnic theater is that it is theater. You can coast just so long on being ethnic. Ultimately, you're the artist, and you must practice your craft. You need polished theatrical technique. You should be judged by the same standards as other theater.

What is distinctive about ethnic theater is that it deals with cultural values. Indian theater is a blending of acting, mime, dance, singing, and instrumentalism. You have to learn about the art forms of many different tribes; thus, the training is rigorous. Not enough Indians are entering the theater. Unfortunately, films and television have re-enforced the stereotype of the Indian as either romantic or a villain. We need scripts that present us as we are. Young Indians must see other Indians in roles they can relate to.

Indian theater is not just songs, dances, and feathers. We're not anthropologists at Red Earth; we don't report cultural patterns. We don't expose sacred dances and ceremonies — that would be sacrilege. We respect the Indian tradition of privacy: Some of the songs are owned by a family or tribe, and you must seek permission before using them. We do want to make a statement about the traditional art forms and cultural values. We present the essence of a dance as a religious experience. Our production *I Give You These Things*, by Hanay Geiogamah, calls for a performance of the Ghost Dance of the Plains Indians in the 1890s. They danced to bring back all the white man had killed. We convey the essence of the dance, the mood, the desperation of the people.

Our performance of *The Changer*, by Bruce Miller, is a retelling of the Skokomish legend of the creation of the world. The mythical character "the Changer" wants to prepare the world for humans. It is a beautiful theatrical piece based on Northwest oral tradition, integrating dance, song, and a cast of incredible characters. Another piece, *Coon Cons Coyote*, by Hanay Geiogamah, is based on a Nez Perce story of the fabulous coyote who represents the con man in all of us. There is gusty, earthy humor, with animals behaving as foolishly as people do. When we laugh at the antics of the animals, we laugh at ourselves.

We're not sociologists at Red Earth, but we do want to show different facets of Indian life and culture. One of our most successful productions, from an artistic standpoint, is *Body Indian*, also by Hanay Geiogamah. Indians came to see it. Many whites were repelled by its harsh truthfulness. The play follows a drunken binge through five scenes. It shows the young as well as the old getting caught up in drunkenness, being reduced by it, and preying on each other. It shows the depths people will go to for alcohol. It's ugly and glaring. The humor is grim; it's self-satire. But that's a double-edged sword. The playwright pulls the audience along, involves them, then suddenly hits them with the grotesqueness of it all. We laugh, but it's really a slap in the face. All Indians have been involved with liquor in some way, if not personally then through a relative or friend. It touches us all.

Theater isn't just an escape. It should make you think. The next time you see someone on the street drunk or panhandling, a light may turn on in your mind. This isn't just a "drunken Indian"; it's a human being. Maybe you'll gain a little humility. Everyone is susceptible, whether it's to liquor or to drugs.

For a creative person, Seattle is a dynamic city. There's tremendous support for the arts. I live in the city now, but I do return to the reservation. I like the change of pace. Many of the people I love are still there. I like to share my life with them and get caught up in theirs. But the city always calls me back.

Theater is my world. Whether as an actor or director, I feel that I must train continually, develop my creativity, grow. Theater is an art form. It guides my life.[51]

Magic Words

In the very earliest time,
when both people and animals lived on earth,
a person could become an animal if he wanted to
and an animal could become a human being . . .

That was the time when words were like magic.
The human mind had mysterious powers.
A word spoken by chance
might have strange consequences.
It would suddenly come alive
and what people wanted to happen could happen —
all you had to do was say it.
Nobody could explain this:
That's the way it was. [52]

                                        Netsilik Eskimo

# Part 3
# Literature

*I remember my father by his songs.*
*This spring he passed on.*
*The songs remember him.*
*They remember.*

*Simon Ortiz*

The poet Wendy Rose writes:

> . . . *my stone spirit song*
> *grows and erupts and laps over the world; my legs roll away*
> *like water on stone and come to where the songs all meet*
> *in ancient matrix, uprooting every spring, and*
> *moving on . . .* [53]

For Native Americans, the tribal past is lost, but not buried. The process of writing is redemptive. Just as early peoples carved legends into stone and, through myth-making, sought to create order out of universal chaos, the contemporary Native American writer turns to the typewriter to make sense out of a world that often seems to lack sensibility. In poetry and prose, the writer captures the unique Indian way of seeing and feeling and being.

> *As my eyes search the prairie*
> *I feel summer in the spring.* [54]

At the very beginning, Simon Ortiz writes, there was no division between experience and expression. The song grew out of the singer's perception of reality. It was an extension of his or her spiritual energy. Today, as in the past, the poet and prose writer respond to an inner voice, but the writer is eclectic, and outside

influences crowd in. Duane Niatum, poet of the Klallam Indians, writes of the parallels between American Indian and Oriental philosophy and arts, which "gave me an interesting hybrid way
of looking at things" and taught him restraint and understatement.
Nevertheless, Niatum writes, "My roots are in the earth and sky
philosophies and arts of my ancestors. As a child, my grandfather
and great-uncle taught me always to humble my soul before the
spiritual reality of things as well as man:"[55]

> *I listen to her heart retreat.*
> *Hyacinths are riding on the windmill of the moon.*
> *I am a stone bedding down in the stream;*
> *She bathes in the unmarked waters of my solitude.*
> *Will she hear my song chanting in the dawn?*[56]

The Native American writer living and working in a white society is faced with a dichotomy. In his autobiography, *Sun Chief*,
the Hopi Don Talayesva recalls the sometimes painful process of
getting "educated" in white man's schools: "I had learned many
English words and could recite part of the Ten Commandments.
I knew how to sleep on a bed, pray to Jesus, comb my hair, eat
with a knife and fork, and use a toilet. I had learned that the
world is round instead of flat, that it is indecent to go naked in the
presence of girls. I had also learned that a person thinks with his
head instead of his heart."

But Talayesva finds himself cut off from tribal ways. An uncle
advises him: "Modern ways help a little; but the whites come and
go, while we Hopi stay forever." And so Talayesva determines to
"become a real Hopi again, to sing the good old Katcina songs, to
feel free to make love without fear of sin or a rawhide," to pay
close attention to his spirit guide and to his dreams.[57]

This idea of blending old worlds and new is a leitmotif that
recurs throughout contemporary native American literature. Like
the visual artist, the writer looks to the oral literature of the tribal
past for the themes, symbols, and imagery that will be re-expressed
in the styles and techniques of today.

In the tribal world, poetry and prose were both secular and

sacred, but only a thin thread separated these two realms, as in this
Omaha creation story:

> At the beginning all things were in the mind of Wa-
> konda. All creatures, including man, were spirits.
> They moved about in space between earth and the stars.
> They were seeking a place where they could come into
> bodily existence . . .[58]

Out of these early legends grew the great tales of supernatural
beings and heroes that served as educational vehicles for passing
on a tribe's mores, moral precepts, and history. The storyteller
was an honored personage in Indian and Eskimo society and was
listened to with respect. In *The Autobiography of a Papago
Woman*, Maria Chona recalls her childhood experience: "My father would . . . start slowly to tell us about how the world began.
This is a story that can be told only in winter when there are no
snakes about . . . Our story about the world is full of songs, and
when the neighbors heard my father singing they would open our
door and step in over the high threshold . . ."[59]

In the myths and hero tales, prose and poetry worked hand in
hand, for the storyteller often flavored his tale with a song. Songs
were designed to bring about fertility and the germination of seeds.
Songs, it was felt, had therapeutic value for healing, rendered
warriors invulnerable, and provided comfort in time of danger or
death. There were lullabies, songs of work, love, rivalry, and
divorce, and those that were vision-inspired. Some were simple
expressions of elation, like this one from the Eskimo:

> . . . *I am crying with joy, lying on the earth.*
> . . . *Ami hai! And up above I see the good caribou*
> *Between the mountains . . .*[60]

Others chronicled tribal history and adventures. More important
than the words was the state of mind evoked by the singer.

Poetry was perceived as power.[61] Words chanted in proper
sequence, accompanied by ritual, were believed to have influence
over natural processes. The desert tribes chanted hypnotically to

bring the much-desired rain.  Eskimo women were thought to possess the power to invoke wild game:

> *Those that sit by the lamp are really strong, for they*
> *know how to call the game to the shore.* [62]

And from the Navajo Night Chant:

> *I am the Slayer of the Alien Gods,*
> *Where'er I roam,*
> *Before me*
> *Forests white are strewn around,*
> *The lightning scatters;*
> *But 'tis I who cause it.* [63]

Poetry was a sort of verbal shorthand, with a few words suggesting intense emotional states.  The abundance of figurative language, archaic expressions, and allusions to events in the tribal past, and the compression of profound philosophical ideas into a few words, made the task of the translator difficult.  Ambiguity was often prized for its own sake.  Secretiveness was cultivated to protect a song from outsiders who might "take away its spirit." Symbolism was prevalent in poetry and storytelling, as it was in the graphic arts.  Words were used impressionistically, one word often suggesting an entire thought process.

Because they are "timeless patterns of sacred forms of seeing and knowing the energy of life," [64] tribal songs speak to us today.  The songs and stories of the past echo in the work of the contemporary Native American writer.  This is not to say that the tone is nostalgic.  In his fine existentialist novel *Winter in the Blood,* James Welch deals with the tragic alienation of young Indians from their tribe and their land.  A few years before this drowning in 1975, the young Canadian Indian poet Sarain Stump wrote:

> *It's with terror, sometimes*
> *That I hear them calling me*
> *But it's the light skip of a cougar*
> *Detaching me from the ground*
> *To leave me alone*

*With my crazy power*
*Till I reach the sun makers*
*And find myself again*
*In a new place.* [65]

The writer today searches for new forms with which to express eternal ideas. Whatever the form, Native American literature remains a celebration of life and of the continuity of all things. Oneida poet Roberta Hill writes:

*. . . We've been traveling since the birth of stars.*
*Let's take a step of simple joy. Let's play flute and sing,*
*watching with glad eyes: star, snow and barren tree.* [66]

## A Wish for Waving Goodbye

Later when the scent of early leaves
from a far-off grove reminds me
how we lay under their applause,
I'll miss touching the corner of your mouth,
(You frowned a little even when you smiled)
but I'll keep driving north, north.
The telephone poles will recede.
Once you waved me gone:
your arm and hand drowned by hills.
I loved you.  It doesn't matter.
Your heart beat against my skin,
and so entangled, we forgot
that this big world is crazed.
The gulls now cry above the wind.
Even awake, I hear them.
Life has opened its door again,
and grace, the largest space we know,
may be just across the threshold.

Roberta Hill, Oneida

# Gerald Vizenor,
# Ojibway/Chippewa writer

*The people of the woodlands, the Anishinabe, "danced to touch the sacred earth and sang with the winds and trees and thundergods to the rhythms of the heart."* [67]

*The literary worlds created by Gerald Vizenor, a member of the Minnesota Chippewa Tribe (White Earth Reservation), are peopled with characters both real and imaginary, sacred and profane, those who praise the oral tradition and sing with the wind and trees, and those who are unable to sing or laugh.*

*Vizenor writes of the way the Indian oral tradition has survived despite attempts to obliterate tribal languages and religions at federal and mission boarding schools on reservations. He directs his ironic wit, his carefully sharpened "wordarrows" at federal bureaucrats, from social workers to officers of the law, who are blind to the needs of Indians but continue to manipulate them. Parody, parable, mythmaking, and dream images mingle in Vizenor's poems and stories and in his books, which include* Tribal Scenes and Ceremonies *and* Wordarrows: Indians and Whites in the New Fur Trade.

*Proude Cedarfair, hero of his recent novel* Darkness in Saint Louis Bearheart, *makes a pilgrimage across the land, finding it barren and in decay. Its people lack the myths and ceremonies with which to celebrate the sacred earth. "Vizenor's nightmare scenario is not so much futuristic as fatalistic; a stern indictment of a culture that has forgotten to love the land."* [68] *But Proude Cedarfair, like his Creator, soars above the world in dreams and sacred visions.*

I don't know what the meaning of my life is. I am not my own biographer. My past is as much a myth and metaphor to me as it is to anyone else. There are some abstract connections — dates, births, rites of passage, deaths, which may have some significance — but the meaning of my life is not determined on a calendar.

As a very young child, I lived with my Anishinabę grandmother and aunts and uncles in a small cold-water apartment near downtown Minneapolis.

> . . . The only personal memory I have from then is my grandmother hiding my nursing bottle, which, she said, I carried around all day clenched between my front teeth. When I was older, she told me between pinches of snuff that she stopped hiding my bottle when I learned the game and started hiding her bottles of whiskey. When she laughed, her round brown cheeks shook and her jumbo stomach jumped up and down under her dress of printed flowers. [69]

My grandmother couldn't remember the exact number of her children. I think most people would regard that as a lapse in memory, even senility. But then she would tell me stories about my father and each of her children — powerful visual experiences. She transformed time with her stories. She passed through calendars, time-binds of the present, and took me into the time of her stories, the time and place of myths.

When I was four years old, my mother, who had remarried following the death of my father, claimed me from my Anishinabe grandmother, and we began a new life.

We lived in a small one-bedroom double bungalow in
north Minneapolis across the street from an un-
developed cemetery where I spent most of my time
alone with my dog. I built dugouts covered with woven
grass and forts in the trees . . .

I entered the third grade at Hamilton Elementary
School and do not remember speaking an audible word
for the whole school year. I had created a life of benign
demons and little people from the woodland of love in
my head. There was no reason then to leave my fan-
tasies for academic prisons and cold rooms . . . I sat at
my little desk seven rows back, never gesturing for recognition or uttering a word. It was a peaceful time. By
the end of the school year I had earned the affectionate
reputation of being a very well behaved slow learner. At
night, in a secret corner of the basement, I would sit
reading parables to my dog.

The calendar events of my childhood are not important. Quan-
tities are forgotten, but personal myths and cultural contradictions
endure. Why are Indians continually obligated to talk with intensity about the details of their squirming on the earth as children?
Writers, social scientists, institutions appropriate that experience
and interpret it according to a preconceived historical scheme.
We are categorized and processed. We are forced to fit into society's notion of what an Indian is, or should be. The white world
has invented the Indian. I rage against the inventions that invali-
date our experiences and our myths. I am not copied from the ar-
tifacts of the past. I am a vibrant human being in this instant, in
this telling.

As a writer, I would like to imagine tribal experience for the
non-Indian, whose frame of reference is very different from ours.
In tribal cultures, human beings are on an equal level with other
life forms. Our origin myths tell of a human transforming himself
into an animal. This is not transcendence or a matter of escaping.
There is no ideal place. This is not a metaphor but a state of
being. A person envisions himself a bear, and he becomes a bear.

Gerald Vizenor. Photo: Peter Denzer.

He steps out of the bonds created by time, and transforms himself
in spirit, with imagination. People work out personal relationships and encounters with nonhuman creatures.

> . . . The benign demons and little woodland people of
> love who lived in my thoughts and fantasies during my
> year of silence in the third grade came to life as real peo-
> ple with real names . . . moving through my head at
> night, nudging me in daydreams along the river and
> leading my visions through boring and repetitious

rhythms of controlled learning in school. They are the
little people who raise the banners of imagination on as-
sembly lines and at cold bus stops in winter. They
marched with me in the service and kept me awake with
humor on duty as a military guard . . .

The little people told me stories when I cracked my
elbow, cut my wrist to the bone, and stood in line waiting to report to my probation officer, and when I was
shot in the lower lip during a real quick-draw gunfight
on a dusty road . . .

Children instinctively understand the idea of transformation.
They communicate with other life forms. They play at achieving
a state of being: "I am a lion," a child will say. He's talked out of
this, taught to be superior to animals. The adult's negative view
of animals enters the child's vocabulary. Such expressions as
"slow as a turtle," "dirty pig," "dumb animal" separate the child
from other animals. People rid themselves and their homes of
anything nonhuman. Screens, sprays, the death blow to anything
that creeps and crawls. They will not tolerate "lower" forms of life
in their domain. And yet cats, lap dogs, and parakeets are per-
missible. Jerry Gerasimo, who teaches college, once asked a class
of adult students what other kind of life they would imagine themselves to be if they could be transformed. To a person they identified with little lap dogs, kitties, domesticated animals that are
cared for and controlled. He was embarrassed because he was the
only wolf there. Gerasimo the wolf scared the hell out of all those
little lap dogs and parakeets.

I remember powerful visual experiences, mostly in connection
with animals and birds. Once I killed a squirrel and it died so
slowly that I could not separate myself from his death.

. . . He fell from the tree and watched me with one
eye. His breath was slower. In his last eye he wanted to
live again, to run free, to hide from me. I knelt beside
him, my face next to his bloody head, my eye close to
his eye, and begged him to forgive me before he died
. . . Not a bird was singing. The leaves were silent

. . . I wept and watched the last of his good life pass
through me in his one remaining eye. I sang a slow
death song in a low voice without words until it was
dark.

My novel *Darkness in Saint Louis Bearheart* deals with this idea
of spiritual transformation. The central character, Proude Cedarfair, transforms himself into a bear through imagination. He
manages to transcend the materialism, hypocrisy, the bizarre sex
and violence that are all around him. Like a shaman, he moves
outside of time and place. He is not willing to die for his vision of
the world. He dignifies life, not death. He is a survivor in a
sacred place.

In the Indian world view, evil cannot be eliminated, for it is a
part of life. One does not declare war against demonic forces.
The idea is to balance adversity with humor; thus the important
function of the clown or fool in tribal cultures.

The idea of tribal trickeries suggests corruption to non-Indians,
but in tribal societies, the "trickster" is a culture hero. In an
Anishinabe story, a trickster confronts an "evil gambler" who
threatens to destroy the people. The trickster knows he must beat
the gambler at his own game, not by destroying him, but by
outwitting him. Through his powers of perception and guile, the
trickster prevails.

It has been said that I play the role of trickster in my writing,
but I do not impose my vision of the world on anyone. I feel a
compulsion to write, to imagine the world around me, and I am
often surprised by what I write.

I am still discovering who I am, the myth in me. Once I was a
ladybird devouring aphids in the tomato plants. Once I made my
home among marigolds at the edge of the garden. I am part crow,
part dragonfly, part squirrel, part bear. I kick the sides of boxes
out. I will not be pinned down. I am flying home in words and
myths.[70]

*Unstoppable*

*Unstoppable, anyway*
*out of place . . . won't sink*
*'til winter.  Like*
*stubborn sun I insist*
*on my peekings*
*and flow whenever*
*the snow turns its face.  I shout the desert*
*into the Arctic, showing up*
*like a bit of lichen, a dry red spread*
*on Mars or something*
*equally incoherent.  I won't go down*
*in being unreal, I won't*
*go down in being unheard.*
                    Wendy Rose, Hopi

# Jamake Highwater,
# Blackfeet writer

*Jamake Highwater's rise in the literary sphere has been meteoric. Beginning college at the age of thirteen, he studied music and comparative literature, and at nineteen was awarded a Ph.D. in cultural anthropology from the University of Chicago, after which he turned to writing.*

*As a commentator and interpreter of American Indian arts and culture, Highwater has achieved prominence. Among his many books are* Song from the Earth: American Indian Painting, Ritual of the Wind: American Indian Ceremonies, Music and Dances, *and* Anpao: An American Indian Odyssey, *winner of the Newbery Honor Award. In addition, he has served as classical music editor of New York's* Soho Weekly News *and contributing editor of* Stereo Review. *Recently, he has been involved in the creation of a television series for the Public Broadcasting Service: "Songs of the Thunderbird: Chronicles from Indian America," for which he is writer, producer, and narrator.*

*Highwater's travels and field work have taken him to many nations throughout the world, and to most Indian reservations in this country. He has served as consultant to the New York State Council on the Arts, and is an honorary member of the White Buffalo Council of American Indians and a member of the National Council of American Indians.*

*Highwater articulates the Indian's aspirations and unique perception of reality.*

In a very real sense, I am the brother of the fox. My whole life revolves around my kinship with four-legged things. I am rooted in the natural world. I'm two people joined into one body. The contradiction doesn't bother me. But people always assume the one they're talking to is the only one there is. That bothers me. There is a little of the legendary Anpao in me, but also a little of Mick Jagger. I stand in both those worlds, not between them. I'm very much a twentieth-century man, and yet I'm a traditional Northern Plains Indian.

I speak eleven languages and can joke in eleven languages. That facility enables me to reach out to people of many different cultures. I'm at home in New York and Europe. My house in Turkey overlooking the Aegean Sea is surrounded by a field of red poppies and golden hay. And yet I need to go home to my origins, to Indian land. There is some place in me where the animal tracks are still fresh.

I'm cautious about my success, and about my visibility. As a tribal person, I've had the rewarding experience of having Native Americans from all tribal backgrounds say, "What you're doing is good." I'm touched by that, because from one side of me, I'm really just standing up and saying my say at a council meeting. And if the elders and the people nod their heads, that's as much achievement as I can expect. But I also live in that other world that gives its recognition in red and yellow lights on buildings. I'm happy if there's a full-page ad for one of my books in the *New York Times*. For if I'm going to make my personal view of the Indian world more visible, then I must do it for Indians and have them nod their heads quietly and say yes, and I must also do it for the kind of billboard mentality that the dominant world lives in, although I do have my priorities and limits.

Jamake Highwater.  Photo: Johan Elbers.

I've always had an enormous regard for the intellect.  Still, I like to go home to my people, who are in touch with the beginning of things.  At home, people are carpenters; some are poets, painters, and teachers; some work on construction jobs.  They are people who perceive the importance of small things that are easily missed by those of us who move much too quickly.  I admire and respect that. People will say, "Shall we take a walk?" We'll walk along quietly. And they'll say, "What is Jimmy Carter thinking?" I'll say, "It's hard for me to say." They'll say, "Did you see the way the moon looked last night?" And we'll talk about that.

In New York City, when I look above the crowds and the carnival atmosphere and comment on the sky and the crowds, people think it's quaint, part of my professional Indian stance.

I was born in the early forties and was raised in northern Montana and southern Alberta, Canada. I'm not enrolled in the Blackfeet tribe, but I spent my first thirteen years among Blackfeet and Cree people. We were very poor, but like most poor people, I didn't know it, didn't know why we always had the same thing for dinner. Our house had a dirt floor. Every spring we scraped the floor, used sheep or calves' blood to refinish it — it's an effective sealer. Many people associate a dirt floor with a primitive existence. Personally, I find asphalt tile very unaesthetic, unappealing. In fact, much of what I see in the middle-class Anglo world is unaesthetic and sterile. Our house was warm in the winter, cool in the summer. We sang, and we were content.

My mother and father are gone now. My father was a founding member of the American Indian Rodeo Association. He was a very good rider. He was also an alcoholic who often fell off his horse. He got a reputation for being very funny, so he became a rodeo clown. My father was a handsome, brave, and wise man, without any education in the traditional Western sense, who worked very hard hoping to build a life for my mother, my brother, and me. But in some strange way he was poisoned with a deep sense of rage about his situation and blamed most of his failures on the fact that he wasn't given chances. I think that probably ninety percent of the time he was right, but ten percent of the time he was fooling himself and, like so many Indians, he didn't take chances. There are those in the dominant culture, too, who forget that although they have been beaten down, they can do something about it. My father, unfortunately, could not.

Filmmakers came to Montana and the Dakotas and hired Native Americans because that was an inexpensive way of getting "extras" for the cowboy-and-Indian crowd scenes. They heard that my dad was a very funny fellow — fell off horses, got on backwards, made people laugh — and so my father became a stunt man in the movies. He died many times for John Wayne. He traveled with the film companies, taking his family along, and I became a carney kid. I have vague recollections of Betty Hutton screaming on a Hollywood set, of seeing fog pumped onto the set of a Charlie Chan movie, a body floating in an indoor ocean. But I didn't know they were movies; I thought it was some sort of adult game with non-Indians playing Indians and non-Orientals playing Orientals (even then I knew we never played ourselves). Weekends we went out to shoot rabbits in the walnut and avocado groves of the San Fernando Valley.

My father was killed in a head-on collision. He certainly didn't feel it, for he was very drunk. My older brother was killed in Korea his second day of combat. My mother, who was an extraordinary person, lived on long enough to see that I had made it in this crazy life of mine. She was a very traditional Indian woman who had no grasp of why I would want to go to a university, study anthropology, and become a writer.

I came to terms with the solemn aspects of life very early. I was always among Indians, for we traveled the powwow circuit. I was always listening to some older person telling stories. They are nameless to me now, and countless, because there were so many. I was introduced to the Indian world as children in my tribe were in the 1870s when we were a nomadic people. I was rootless, yet connected to a vital tradition. The elders talked to me and gave me a sense of the meaning of my existence.

I talk and think as a poet, but I don't want to perpetuate the romantic notion of the Indian as watching chipmunks his entire life, waiting to see which side of the tree the moss grows on. For the Indian, art is not reserved for a leisure class, as it is in Anglo society. It is part of our fundamental way of thinking. We are an aesthetic people. Most primal people are. We represent a constant chord that's been resounding ever since man began. While those Cro-Magnon people in the caves of southern France (at least according to Western mentality) should have been out worrying about the great likelihood that they wouldn't survive, they were building scaffolds fifty or sixty feet high and with tiny oil lamps were painting the ceilings of their caves with marvelous magical images. These images were an implicit and important part of their lives. For us, this aesthetic reality is a continuous process. The kiva murals of the Hopi and the Mimbres pottery rival the finest accomplishments of Western art. This idea of life as art is part of being Indian. It's not quaint or curious or charming. It's fundamental, like plowing a field. There's great beauty in plowing a field.

The twentieth century is rediscovering what it is to be a primal person, to be human. It has finally become apparent that Indians have something to contribute, that we're one of the last reservoirs on earth for this aesthetic mentality — not through our isolation, but through our tenaciousness. We have something urgent to say and something vital to be. But on the other hand, that doesn't mean that we are incapable of being brutes or sexist, being insensitive and drinking too much. We are who we are; we're people, with many facets to our nature. We know how to live in the twentieth century. Because if we didn't, we'd be like the dinosaur or the dodo bird — we'd be gone.

I think Indians have become a metaphor for a larger idea. We are building bridges toward cultures. Some people in white society are also building bridges toward us, and they sometimes join together. That means that it's possible for everyone to find the Indian in himself. It's a kind of sensibility that I'm talking about.

Indians have always had the greatest facility of all: the power of transformation. It's the thing white society is most stubborn about. They won't let people change, except perhaps nuns, priests, and popes who take on a mystical relation to the deity. Women are permitted to change their names and loyalties, but only because they're not considered much to begin with. It's sad. We are committed like prisoners to our identities in the Western world. We cannot become who we believe ourselves to be. Indians, on the other hand, transform themselves into different

beings in ceremonies.  We go through initiation, wear special garments and become kachinas, masked figures who impersonate deities.  Indian and non-Indian dancers don't just do a dance; they
become the dance.  All dancers are "Indians."  Artists are all Indians, too.  This capacity to believe in transformation is what makes
art urgent.  Because art is essentially a form of transformation.

What were my doorways into Western culture?  How did I get a
Ph.D., and why did I want one?  How is it that I was reading
Proust when I was nine, and listening to Edgard Varèse's music?
Well, it's all because of a woman named Alta Black, my teacher
and great friend from the time I was seven or eight.  A white
woman, she came West in a covered wagon.  So outrageous for
her time, she learned the Blackfeet language so she could teach
Indian children.  When I was eight, she gave me an old typewriter
and a book and said I was to learn to type because I would be a
writer.

I ran around with a bunch of hostile Indian boys.  I was a big
kid, violent, a sort of gang leader.  We beat up white kids who we
felt insulted us.  But Alta Black believed in me.  She continued as
my teacher through the sixth grade and tutored me when I entered
the university at thirteen.  I grew a mustache at thirteen and ran
around in a trench coat.  As my spiritual guide, she introduced
me to the whole of Western culture.  At the end, when she was
dying of cancer, she wrote me her death song.  She's gone now,
but I'm not sure that Alta Black is dead.

All I've done is carry out my instructions.  All I really am is
what I was made to be.  The talent is in me — I don't know
where it came from.  When I write, I go away for hours at a time.
I don't know where I've been or who does the writing.  I have to
give myself up to it entirely.  I'm a technician.  I use a typewriter.
But I can't take credit for my work.  In some way I feel I'm just a
conduit.  You have to be a very good conduit, like a good Amati
violin, but I think someone else plays me.

As Indians, we are extensions of a people.  I am not a person, I
am a people, a Blackfeet.  I am one aspect of a rainbow, part of a
whole spectrum.  I don't make any sense by myself.  I only make

sense in terms of the continuity of the whole. I think this is true of all people, but some of us have lost touch with it.

I care what happens to Indian people. I feel that we are a spiritual body. We are dreamers; we believe in dreams. We are brought together by the beautiful. But the word beauty has been distorted. For the Native American there can be great beauty in a cypress tree that's been lashed and twisted by the wind. There is beauty in being ourselves.

I'm concerned about what happens to young Indian boys and girls who are the way I was. I'm involved anonymously with Indian political and social service organizations — that's part of my tribal heritage. If what has happened to me means anything, it means that we can be transformed. We are like clay. With help and guidance, we can shape ourselves into absolutely anything. We can become what we believe in. It takes courage. After all, we are all going to die. How much better to give back a plump, ripe fruit to the earth that it can grow on, than something that's hardly developed.

That's the important thing, to give something back to the earth.[71]

*Death Song of a Yokuts Song Maker*

*All my life*
  *I have been seeking,*
  *Seeking!*

# Simon Ortiz,
# Acoma poet

*It is November in Acoma, the sunlit, hilltop pueblo near Albuquerque, New Mexico, where Simon Ortiz spent the first twenty years of his life. There is a chill in the air. Ortiz observes the piñon trees, the mountains nearby. He thinks of the deer he will soon hunt and sings in Acoma. Translated, the words mean:*

> *My helping guide, Mountain Lion Hunting Spirit Friend, in this direction to this point bring the Deer to me.* Wahyuuhuunah wahyuuhuu huu nai ah.

*Ortiz enters into an active relationship with Mountain Lion, the spirit friend and guide, and with Deer.*[72] *If the song and the ritual are performed well, his prayer will be answered. With such a prayer song, chanted by his ancestors for countless generations, Ortiz participates in the ethic and the spirit that guide the universe.*

*Song, at the very beginning, was experience, Ortiz has written. Language permits him the vision with which to see, to know himself. It is a road from inside himself to the outside, and from outside of himself to inside. "It is always a continuing motion, never ending."*[73]

*Ortiz has been a baker's helper, clerk, soldier in the U.S. Army, college student, laborer, and is currently an instructor in Native American Studies at the University of New Mexico. Major publica-*

*tions include* Gong for the Rain, *1976;* A Good Journey, *1977;*
Howbah Indians, *1978; and a collection of poetry and narratives
for his children,* Rainy Dawn and Raho Nez.

*The stories of Simon Ortiz possess the directness and color of
traditional oral narratives. His poetry, though at times laced with
sardonic wit, flows with the musical cadence of song. In all his
writing he seeks to reconcile conventional Pueblo wisdom with the
perplexing realities of contemporary Native American life.*

▬▬▬

My first love is the Indian oral tradition, storytelling. I have put
some of the stories into verse form so that they look and read like
poems. But I'm more concerned with the way people speak and
think than with style or form.

> *After I got out of the back*
> *of a red pickup truck,*
> *I walked for about a mile*
> *and met three goats, two sheep and a lamb*
> *by the side of the road.*
> *I was wearing a bright red wool cap*
> *pulled over my ears,*
> *and I suppose they thought I was maybe weird*
> *because they were all ears and eyes.*
> *I said, "Yaahteh, my friends.*
> *I'm from Acoma, just passing through."*
> *The goat with the bell jingled it*
> *in greeting a couple of times.*
> *I could almost hear the elder sheep*
> *telling the younger, "You don't see*
> *many Acoma poets passing through here."* [74]

My narrations are extensions of hundreds of thousands of years of
songmaking. Some are old, some are new. The songs evolve; the
individual adapts them for today. But the rhythms, the nuances,

come from the same source as the oral tradition. I humbly acknowledge the source.

My richest inspiration as a writer comes from love. There is also fear, frustration, and anger, but there is an enduring attempt to keep on loving the land.

> *and the land was a pretty woman*
> *smiling at us*
> *looking at her.*

And the people. This is passed on in Indian society through our songs and ceremonies. This is how the people express who they are, what they know, the continuance of their tradition. I write for those I love, for my son, Raho, and my daughter, Rainy Dawn.

Simon Ortiz. Photo: Evelina Zuni.

*Rainy*
*daughter dark eyes*
*touch wind quiver*
*the inwards of mountain power*
*full flow*
*know the innate tension*
*that is your life*
*in stones leaves insects*
*lights in frost crystals;*
*simple words I wish*
*for you*
*ours to share.*

I write for my father. He was one of the elders of the Antelope People, who are in charge of the spiritual practice and philosophy of our people, the Acoma. It was his responsibility to see that things continue for us in the way that they have since time began. In that sense, he was a thousand-year-old man.

> My father is a small man, in fact, almost tiny . . .
> He's very wiry, and his actions are wiry. Smooth, al-
> most tight motions, but like currents in creek water or
> an oak branch in a mild mountain wind. His face is
> even formed like that. Rivulets from the sides of his
> forehead, squints of his eyes, down his angular face and
> under his jaw . . . His hair is . . . the color of distant
> lava cliffs.[75]

My father was a woodcarver, and a songmaker.

Many of my songs and narrations deal with contemporary issues. So many American artists isolate themselves from what is going on. They're in an unreal position, alienated from the dynamic forces of change in this society. Indian people have been educated within the American school system to accept its values and standards. Some of us have said, almost in imitation of those values, "I'm an artist. I'm not political." Indians can't afford to insulate themselves behind walls. Our literature comes out of a long historical process that has at times been destructive. We have survived. Our very existence is evidence of that. Our continued survival as a people means being conscious that this has been a political struggle.

Americans would like to believe in the myth of the "passive Indian." It was official government policy to exterminate Indians in the eighteenth and nineteenth centuries. Then, when that was no longer politically feasible, assimilation became the objective — to turn Indian people into "whites." Indians were never passive. They resisted this steadfast policy of cultural genocide. There are still those who would annihilate us, whether politically, socially, or culturally. This is threatening for Indian people and, potentially, for all people. Such neofascism endangers everyone. But most people are complacent.

> *Beneath the cement foundations*
> *of the motel, the ancient spirits*
> *of the People conspire sacred tricks . . .*
>
> *The American passersby*
> *get out of their hot, stuffy cars*
> *at evening, pay their money wordlessly,*
> *and fall asleep without benefit of dreams.*
> *The next morning, they get up,*
> *dress automatically, brush their teeth,*
> *get in their cars and drive away.*
> *They haven't noticed that the cement*
> *foundations of the motor hotel*
> *are crumbling, bit by bit.*
>
> *The ancient spirits tell stories*
> *and jokes and laugh and laugh.*

I want to deal with the realities people don't admit to. Systematically, and by design, the American school system has prevented Indian people from thinking for themselves. Most of our schools have been dominated by the Bureau of Indian Affairs, which fears loss of control over our minds, our communities. We the people have a responsibility to remember our history. We must be concerned about social change and involved in the process.

To a large extent, Indians are victims of the American mercantile mentality. The media still perpetuates the "wild Indian" stereotype. Pseudo-Indian dances that cheapen our culture are staged for the entertainment and profit of non-Indians. Indian art is still a curiosity, bringing high prices but little awareness of the culture that produces it. White-owned industries derive profits from oil, gas, coal mining, and uranium on Indian land.

> *What the hell are you doing to this land!*
> *My grandfather hunted here, prayed,*
> *dreamt; one day there was a big jolt,*
> *flame, and then silence,*
> *just the clouds forming.*

Water is the lifeblood of the Southwest tribes; rivers needed for irrigation are diverted by the energy companies. The air is polluted, plant life is destroyed. Indian people are threatened with the loss of all their resources to the states and federal government — the Department of the Interior, the U.S. Army Corps of Engineers, and the Department of Agriculture, acting in collusion with the multinational corporations.

Most white Americans are not aware of the extent to which Indians are exploited, or do not want to know, for racism is thoroughly embedded in the American consciousness. Indian organizations are working continually to bring the truth out into the open, but it's difficult to mobilize successfully the many diverse groups within the Indian community. Furthermore, government and industry are allied with the media. They have the money and the power to silence and even suppress Indian protest.

I served in the army at the beginning of the Vietnam War — a war that almost destroyed a people and desecrated their land. This country has waged war against its own people, against Indians who view land and life as sacred. This, too, is a sacrilege. You can love your country and still express dissent. Perhaps this is the deepest form of love.

From childhood in Indian society we are taught to love our grandparents, our parents, our children, ourselves, our home, our land. We are taught to have compassion for black people, white people, for all human beings. Indian society is very structured. Each of us is taught to think of order and what will benefit society. The individual's role is ordained. One is valued for one's contribution to the society. *"Hahno Gowtseniah,"* we say in Acoma — it is for the sake of the people. There is a set of principles at the core of tribal life and at the core of being human. We try to follow these, despite the opposition.

Cooperation is central to the dynamic of the Indian social system. The capitalistic system encourages material acquisition and stepping on others: This is alien to Indian people. The pressures in American society to climb the ladder and get to the top are overwhelming.

We are at times discouraged.

> *Dreams gather quickly*
> *Like spring crows*
> *and they scatter.*

We have experienced few victories. There has been much to mourn. And yet we persist. Just being alive is a victory.

I've lived on reservations, I've been to schools and colleges, I've been in the army, I've been in jail, I've been an alcoholic. I don't drink anymore, but it's a real struggle. I have feared death, and I have feared life. There are scars on my face, on my heart, on my mind. But I continue to love, to teach, and to write.

> *It's a duty with me,*
> *I know, to find the horizons,*
> *and I keep on walking on the ocean's edge,*
> *looking for things in the dim light.*

Americans always expect life to continue in the familiar pattern. But it doesn't. Things change. People we love die. Their work may be unfinished, but life goes on. We carry on what they started. There is the process of regeneration.[76]

> *I remember my father by his songs*
> *This spring he passed on.*
> *The songs remember him.*
> *They remember. . .*

# Leslie Silko,
## Laguna poet and novelist

*Etched into the consciousness of Leslie Silko, one of the most pro-*
*found and lyrical writers today, is the landscape of the Southwest-*
*ern pueblos where, among the arroyos and dusty mesas, she was*
*born and nurtured:*

> *. . . Where I come from is like this*
> *the warmth, the fragrance, the silence*
> *Blue sky and rainclouds in the distance*
> *we ride together*
> *past cliffs with stories and songs*
> *painted on rock*
> *700 years ago.*[77]

*Since publication of her first short story in the* New Mexico
Quarterly *in 1969, Silko's finely crafted poetry and prose have been*
*widely acclaimed. In 1974 she received a poetry award from the*
Chicago Review *and in that year published* Laguna Woman, *her*
*first collection of poems. Her work has appeared in* The Man to
Send Rain Clouds, Voices of the Rainbow, Carriers of the Dream
Wheel, I Am the Fire of Time, *and other collections.*
   Ceremony, *Leslie Silko's remarkable first novel, published in*
*1977, has been hailed as "exceptional in its interweaving of indi-*
*vidual and cosmic fates, a drama framed by the polarities of tradi-*
*tional Laguna and contemporary Western metaphysics."*[78]  *It*
*deals with witchery, the idea in old Laguna stories that the forces of*

*evil are at large.  After participating in the white man's violation
of the land and the Japanese people, Tayo, a shell-shocked Indian
veteran of World War II, returns home to find destructiveness all
around him.  Whites assault the land for its commercially valuable
natural resources.  Internalizing the white man's view that Indians
are worthless, alienated from land, family, and traditions, Tayo
and his friends do battle with each other and themselves.  In startling counterpoint, the malignancy within and around Tayo con-
trasts with the redemptive powers of the land, the old songs, and
ancient holistic medicine.  It is a work of startling honesty and
beauty.*

*Ms. Silko's newest book is* Storyteller, *which blends short fiction
and poetry.*

I was born in 1948 in Albuquerque, New Mexico.  I grew up in
the house at Laguna where my father was born.  The house was
built ninety years ago with rock and adobe mortar walls two feet
thick.  Outside there was a great old mountain cottonwood tree,
five feet around at its base.  Our house was next to my great-
grandmother's house.  My mother had to work, so I spent most of
my time with my great-grandma, following her around her yard
while she watered the hollyhocks and blue morning glories.

When I got older I carried the coal bucket inside for her.  Her
name was Maria Anaya and she was born in Paguate Village,
north of Old Laguna.  She came to Laguna when she married my
great-grandfather, who was a white man.  She took care of me and
my sisters, and she told us about how things were when she was a
little girl.

*Some white men came to Acoma and Laguna a hundred years ago
and they fought over Acoma land and Laguna women, and even now
some of their descendants are howling in
the hills southeast of Laguna.*

Leslie Silko. Photo: Denny Carr. Courtesy of Viking Press.

The white men who came to the Laguna Pueblo Reservation and married Laguna women were the beginning of the half-breed Laguna people like my family, the Marmon family. The Marmons are very controversial, even now, but I think that people watch us more closely than they do full bloods or white people. In the long run we aren't much different from other Laguna families.

I suppose at the core of my writing is the attempt to identify what it is to be a half-breed or mixed-blooded person, what it is to grow up neither white nor fully traditional Indian. It is for this reason that I hesitate to say that I am representative of Indian poets or Indian people, or even Laguna people. I am only one human being, one Laguna woman.

My great-grandfather came to Laguna after the Civil War in the 1870s. He got to Albuquerque by train, then rode on horseback to Laguna. His legs and behind were so blistered, he had to walk the last twenty miles. He was a surveyor, had a contract with the government, and laid out all the bench marks around here.

Climbing around the hills, you'll find those old, tarnished bench marks to this day.

My mother was born in Montana and her family came from a Plains Indian tribe, but she never knew which one for sure. My father stayed on the reservation and helped my grandpa and grandma with the little grocery store they had. My father was once elected treasurer of the pueblo of Laguna, but being a Marmon, it wasn't easy to get along very well politically.

Look where all the Marmon houses are here by the river, down below the village. I always thought there was something symbolic about that — we're on the fringe of things. The river's just a short walk from here, and I was always attracted to it as a kid. I knew it was a small river, and I didn't make any great demands on it. It was a great place to go and play in the mud and splash around. There are willows and tamarack, and there are always stories. You just hear them. I guess from the beginning there was the idea that the river was kind of a special place where all sorts of things could go on. I got stuck in the sand down there once, and my grandma pulled me out and switched me. But I kept going back, even when I was twelve, thirteen, fourteen — except by then my idea of the possibilities for the river had grown. I saw beyond catching minnows and frogs; I began to realize the possibilities that the people have forever realized. The river was a place to meet boyfriends and lovers. I used to wander around down there and try to imagine walking around the bend and just happening to stumble upon some beautiful man.

> *that time*
> *in the sun*
> *beside the Rio Grande.*

> *voice of the mourning dove*
> *calls*
> *    long ago  long ago*
> *remembering the lost one*
> *remembering the love . . .*
> *man of Sun*

> *came to riverwoman*
> *and in the sundown wind*
>    *he left her*
>       *to sing*
>          *for rainclouds swelling in the northwest sky*
>          *for rainsmell on pale blue winds*
>                               *from China.*


I finally put the two together: the adolescent longings and the old stories, plus the stories around Laguna at the time about people who did, in fact, use the river as a meeting place. Then there were the warning stories, like the one about the old man who lost a team of horses in the quicksand. And the stories that incorporated you and your family into them. The river was a sort of focal point bringing all of that together. I see now that the ideas and dreams and fears and wonderful and terrible things that I expected might happen around the river were part of an identity that the stories had made for it. By going to the river, I was stepping into that identity.

It's stories that make this into a community. There have to be stories. That's how you know; that's how you belong; that's how you know you belong.

Stories were important for us Marmons because we are a mixed-breed family. The clan system was still maintained, although not in the same form it would have been if we were full-blood. The process went on, but it changed slightly for us. The Lagunas told stories about these mixed-blood people, half-breeds who had gone outside Laguna, and of the outsiders who had come in. They told about the wild, roguish things they did.

In a sense, this separate identity gave me latitude. It opened up possibilities. A very different set of possibilities was open to Simon Ortiz, a full-blood Acoma man whose father was deeply involved in the community religious life. There was a whole different set of stories and expectations for him that in a way may have constricted him.

Many contemporary poets are "rescuing" songs and stories from old Bureau of American Ethnology reports, and their efforts are often thought of as the Native American oral tradition. I feel that I'm working from a more vital source:

> *This woman loved a man*
> *and she breathed to him*
> > *her damp earth song.*
>
> *I am haunted by this story*
> *I remember it in cottonwood leaves*
> > *their fragrance in the shade.*
>
> *I remember it in the wide blue sky*
> *when the rainsmell comes with the wind.*

For a long time I was self-conscious about not knowing the Laguna language better than I do. I expressed that in a poem about my grandfather. I always had the feeling that he died too soon. But I was never tempted to use the stories just the way the anthropologists reported them.

In 1930, [anthropologist] Elsie Clews Parsons wrote off Laguna as a lost cause. She said it had no kiva and that it was dead. And the same went for the "oral tradition."

From the time I was little I was hearing, and you still can. There's a kind of continuum, despite Elsie Clews Parsons. It's like last year at Laguna Feast they had a trash fight. There were some Navajos down at the trash pile, and they had a fight. Every year at Laguna Feast there are these incidents. I always loved stories about them so much that the things in the anthropological reports looked dead and alien.

I started writing a story about ethnologists continually milking their "informants." When I started to write, I started to laugh. I never did get past the first encounter. This Charlie Coyote type is starting to size up the anthropologist. When he leaves, someone says to Coyote, "What'd you tell him that for? Those are outrageous lies."

When I write a poem, it just starts to come together. The one about the Coyote chain is based on an old story. The old men would sit around the stove, and they'd say, "The storyteller cannot begin. The storyteller cannot tell stories unless there's some parched corn or piñons at the least." So someone would have to jump up and get this before the storyteller would begin. The old version of the story is very long, because the people have a lot of time, or they make time to talk. A good story was one that would last long enough. It was one that has all kinds of details, gestures, and facial expressions. I condensed the old story of Toe'osh, Coyote, for my poem:

> *They were after the picnic food*
> *That the special dancers left*
> *down below the cliff.*
> *And Toe'osh and his cousins hung themselves*
> *down over the cliff*
> *holding each other's tail in their mouth*
> *   making a coyote chain*
> *until someone in the middle farted*
> *and the guy behind him opened his*
> *mouth to say "What Stinks?" and they*
> *all went tumbling down, like that.*

The longer version is really funny. Coyote comes over to the edge of this mesa and peeks over and he sees these dancers. They're from a dance society that has died out; what they were doing down there was kind of mysterious. They had laid out all the food that they were going to eat when they got done dancing. The story is kind of cinematographic. Coyote peeks down from way up high on the mesa, sees the food, and says, "Mmmm, wow, it looks good. But it's way down there." Then he calls his cousins, "Ooooh, ooooh," and when they gather, he says he has this brilliant idea about the coyote chain. They're hesitant, afraid of falling, but he reassures them that everything's gonna go fine. I've thought about this a lot. The one thing he hadn't taken into consideration happens.

The witch stories fit into contemporary Indian oral tradition, and I've used some in my novel *Ceremony*. Witchcraft stories are

rare in Laguna.   Simon Ortiz says that when a community is
together, fairly orderly, when the livestock and the food supply is
good and nothing drastic has happened to shake the people's faith,
then there's not much talk of witchcraft.   When it does occur, the
whole community deals with it.   It's different with the Navajo.
Witchcraft activity is incessant.   The whole time I was in Chinle
and Lukachuchai, it was so-and-so's got a rash on his hands because he did this, and so-and-so wrecked her car because so-and-so
caused it.

In the novel, I've tried to go beyond any specific kind of Laguna
witchery or Navajo witchery, and to begin to see witchery as a
metaphor for the destroyers, or the counterforce, that force which
counters vitality and birth.   The counterforce is destruction and
death.   I tried to get away from talking about good and evil, and to
return to an old, old, old way of looking at the world that I think is
valid — the idea of balance, that the world was created with these
opposing forces.

Tayo returns from World War II with nightmares about killing
Japanese soldiers.   White medicine is ineffectual in treating his
war hysteria, for it does not acknowledge the witchery, the malig-
nant force that has been unleashed on the world.   It's the struggle
between the force and the counterforce.   I try to take it beyond
any particular culture or continent, because that's such a bullshit
thing — it's all Whitey's fault.   That's too simplistic, mindless.
In fact, Tayo is warned that *they* try to encourage people to focus
on certain people or groups, to blame them for everything.   Another name for the counterforce is "the manipulators," those who
create nothing, merely take what is around.   Inevitably, when
there's nothing left for Tayo, he turns to a Navajo medicine man
for healing.   It is a ceremony that started long ago, and goes on
and on.

The oral tradition is going strong at Laguna.   The good old
adultery stories are better than ever and much more intricate,
because now everyone has indoor plumbing, so that you no longer
have that excuse to go out — which was a pretty good one.

At the end of my novel, the old woman says, "I'm getting too

old to even get excited about the goings-on around here anymore.
It's all beginning to sound like I've heard all those stories before" — at which point she goes to sleep.[79]

*Chant of the Yokuts Indians*

*My words are tied in one*
*with the great mountains,*
*with the great rocks,*
*with the great trees,*
*in one with my body*
*and my heart . . .*
*And you day,*
*And you night!*
*All of you see me*
*one with this world.*[80]

# N. Scott Momaday,
## Kiowa poet and novelist

*An essayist, poet, novelist, and academician, N. Scott Momaday has strayed far from his boyhood origins on an Oklahoma reservation. However, the land has left its imprint on his imagination and his work.*

> *I have walked in a mountain meadow bright with Indian paintbrush, lupine, and wild buckwheat, and I have seen high in the branches of a lodgepole pine the male pine grosbeak, round and rose-colored, its dark, striped wings nearly invisible in the soft, mottled light. And the uppermost branches of the tree seemed very slowly to ride across the blue sky . . .* [81]

*Momaday was born in 1934 in Lawton, Oklahoma, the son of artist Al Momaday and writer Natachee Scott Momaday. In his writing, and in his drawings and paintings of recent years, he pays homage to his heritage. His first art exhibit was held at the University of North Dakota Art Gallery in 1979.*

*Momaday's published works include the Pulitzer Prize–winning novel* House Made of Dawn, *1968;* The Way to Rainy Mountain, *1969;* Angle of Geese and Other Poems, *1974;* Gourd Dancer, *a book of poems illustrated by the author in 1976;* The Names, *in the same year; and the screenplay for the Frank Waters novel* The Man Who Killed the Deer.

*Abel, the Indian protagonist of Momaday's* House Made of Dawn, *is a young man nourished among the wheat fields and canyons of the Southwestern pueblos, taught by his grandfather to revere the sun, the rain, "the house made of dawn." Suddenly catapulted into the white man's war, he is unprepared for the brutality of twentieth-century technology:*

> *Then, through the falling leaves, he saw the machine. It rose up behind the hill, black and massive, looming there in front of the sun. He saw it swell, deepen, and take shape on the skyline, as if it were some upheaval of the earth, the eruption of stone and eclipse, and all about it the glare, the cold perimeter of light, throbbing with leaves. For a moment it seemed apart from the land . . . He was shaking violently, and the machine bore down upon him, came close, and passed him by . . .* [82]

*Momaday cautions Indians not to get caught up in white society's "marketplace mentality," but rather to remember the vision of their forefathers. In a speech to a group of Indian scholars he said, "We may be perfectly sure of where we are in relation to the supermarket and the next coffee break, but I doubt that any of us knows where he is in relation to the stars and to the solstices."* [83]

*Momaday's autobiographical prose poem* The Way to Rainy Mountain *is a poetic vision quest recapturing the spirit of his ancestors who "dared to imagine and determine who they were." In this book, past and present, poetry and history, myth and memory intermingle as Momaday tells us where he came from and who he is.*

A single knoll rises out of the plain in Oklahoma, north and west of the Wichita Range. For my people, the Kiowas, it is an old landmark, and they gave it the name Rainy Mountain. The hardest weather in the world is there. Winter brings blizzards, but tornadic winds arise in the spring, and in summer the prairie is an anvil's edge. The grass turns brittle and brown, and it cracks beneath your feet. There are green belts along the rivers and creeks, linear groves of hickory and pecan, willow and witch hazel. At a distance in July or August the steaming foliage seems almost to writhe in fire . . .

I returned to Rainy Mountain in July. My grandmother had died in the spring, and I wanted to be at her grave. She had lived to be very old and at last infirm. Her only living daughter was with her when she died, and I was told that in death her face was that of a child . . .

Her name was Aho, and she belonged to the last culture to evolve in North America. Her forebears came down from the high country in western Montana nearly three centuries ago. They were a mountain people, a mysterious tribe of hunters whose language has never been positively classified in any major group. In the late seventeenth century they began a long migration to the south and east. It was a journey toward the dawn, and it led to a golden age. Along the way the Kiowas were befriended by the Crows, who gave them the culture and religion of the Plains. They acquired horses, and their ancient nomadic spirit was suddenly free of the ground. They acquired Tai-me, the sacred Sun Dance doll, from that moment the object and symbol of their worship, and so shared in the divinity of the sun. Not least, they acquired the sense of destiny, therefore courage and pride. When they entered upon the southern Plains they had been transformed. No longer were they slaves to the simple necessity of survival; they were a lordly and dangerous society of fighters and thieves, hunters and priests of the sun. According to their origin myth, they entered the world through a hollow log. From one point of view, their migration was the fruit of an old prophecy, for indeed they emerged from a sunless world.

Although my grandmother lived out her long life in the shadow of Rainy Mountain, the immense landscape of the continental interior lay like memory in her blood. She could tell of the Crows, whom she had never seen, and of the Black Hills, where she had never been. I wanted to see in reality what she had seen more perfectly in the mind's eye, and traveled fifteen hundred miles to begin my pilgrimage . . .

A dark mist lay over the Black Hills, and the land was like iron. At the top of a ridge I caught sight of Devil's Tower upthrust against the gray sky as if in the birth of time the core of the earth had broken through its crust and the motion of the world was begun . . .

My grandmother had a reverence for the sun, a holy regard that now is all but gone out of mankind. There was a wariness in her, and an ancient awe. She was a Christian in her later years, but she had come a long way about, and she never forgot her birthright. As a child she had been to the Sun Dances; she had taken part in those annual rites, and by them she had learned the restoration of her people in the presence of Tai-me . . .

Now that I can have her only in memory, I see my grandmother in the several postures that were peculiar to her: standing at the wood stove on a winter morning and turning meat in a great iron skillet; sitting at the south window, bent above her beadwork, and afterward, when her vision failed, looking down for a long time into the fold of her hands; going out upon a cane, very slowly, as she did when the weight of age came upon her; praying. I remember her most often at prayer. She made long, rambling prayers out of suffering and hope, having seen many things. I was never sure that I had the right to hear, so exclusive were they of all mere custom and company. The last time I saw her, she prayed standing by the side of her bed at night, naked to the waist, the light of a kerosene lamp moving upon her dark skin. Her long, black hair, always drawn and braided in the day, lay upon her shoulders and against her breasts like a shawl. I do not speak Kiowa, and I never understood her prayers, but there was something inherently sad in the sound, some merest hesitation upon the syllables of sorrow. She began in a high and descending pitch, exhausting her breath to silence; then again and again — and always the same intensity of effort, of something that is, and is not, like urgency in the human voice. Transported so in the

N. Scott Momaday.  Photo: Jim Kalett.  Courtesy of Harper & Row,
Inc.

dancing light among the shadows of her room, she seemed beyond
the reach of time.  But that was illusion; I think I knew then that I
should not see her again.

Houses are like sentinels in the plain, old keepers of the weather
watch.  There, in a very little while, wood takes on the appearance of great age.  All colors wear soon away in the wind and rain,
and then the wood is burned gray and the grain appears and the

nails turn red with rust. The windowpanes are black and opaque; you imagine there is nothing within, and indeed there are many ghosts, bones given up to the land. They stand here and there against the sky, and you approach them for a longer time than you expect. They belong in the distance; it is their domain.

Once there was a lot of sound in my grandmother's house, a lot of coming and going, feasting and talk. The summers there were full of excitement and reunion. The Kiowas are a summer people; they abide the cold and keep to themselves, but when the season turns and the land becomes warm and vital, they cannot hold still; an old love of going returns upon them. The aged visitors who came to my grandmother's house when I was a child were made of lean and leather, and they bore themselves upright. They wore great black hats and bright ample shirts that shook in the wind. They rubbed fat upon their hair and wound their braids with strips of colored cloth. Some of them painted their faces and carried the scars of old and cherished enmities. They were an old council of warlords, come to remind and be reminded of who they were . . .

There were frequent prayer meetings, and great nocturnal feasts. When I was a child I played with my cousins outside, where the lamplight fell upon the ground and the singing of the old people rose up around us and carried away into the darkness. There were a lot of good things to eat, a lot of laughter and surprise. And afterwards, when the quiet returned, I lay down with my grandmother and could hear the frogs away by the river and feel the motion of the air.

Now there is a funereal silence in the rooms, the endless wake of some final word. The walls have closed in upon my grandmother's house. When I returned to it in mourning, I saw for the first time in my life how small it was. It was late at night, and there was a white moon, nearly full. I sat for a long time on the stone steps by the kitchen door. From there I could see out across the land; I could see the long rows of trees by the creek, the low light upon the rolling plains, and the stars of the Big Dipper. Once I looked at the moon and caught sight of a strange thing. A cricket had perched upon the handrail, only a few inches away from me. My line of vision was such that the creature filled the moon like a fossil. It had gone there, I thought, to live and die, for there, of all places, was its small definition made whole and eternal. A warm wind rose up and purled like the longing within me.

The next morning I awoke at dawn and went out on the dirt road to Rainy Mountain. It was already hot, and the grasshoppers began to fill the air. Still, it was early in the morning, and the birds sang out of the shadows. The long yellow grass on the mountain shone in the bright light, and a scissortail hied above the land. There, where it ought to be, at the end of a long and legendary way, was my grandmother's grave. Here and there on the dark stones were ancestral names. Looking back once, I saw the mountain and came away.[84]

*. . . . tribal dream songs . . .*
*more beautiful than flowers*

*dream children touching the earth again*
*with gnarled fingers*

*the scars of reservation life*
*turning under with age*

*the sacred earth remembers*
*every flower*

*grandchildren following*
*clumsy and clover-stained*
*tasting the rain*
*singing*
*the world will change*

Gerald Vizenor

# Acknowledgments

This book has been long in evolving. There have been friends and advisors along the way. I am especially grateful to:

Simon Ortiz for use of the line "This Song Remembers" from a song, © 1978, by Simon Ortiz.

Linda Crawford of the Raven Gallery in Minneapolis, for information and inspiration.

Judy Vick, University of Minnesota News Service, and Mike Oker, art director of the Native American Center, Minneapolis, for making materials available.

Ruth Ballard for background information in connection with her husband's oral history.

My father, Harvey J. Bresler; Nancy Goldstein; Judith Yellin; and Joan Calof for reading portions of the manuscript.

Carl Gawboy and Gerald Vizenor, Department of American Indian Studies, University of Minnesota, for their informed critique and honest feedback.

Bonnie Wallace, chairwoman, Department of American Indian Studies, Augsburg College, for support and encouragement.

For any errors and omissions, I accept full responsibility.


The author is grateful to the following for permission to reprint material in this book:

Peter Blue Cloud for excerpt from "A New Roundhouse: Northern California," from *Akwesasne Notes*, Spring 1978. Copyright © 1978 by Peter Blue Cloud.

Dorothy Eber for excerpts from *Pitseolak: Pictures out of My Life*, from recorded interviews by Dorothy Eber, University of Washington Press. Copyright © 1971 by Dorothy Eber.

Education Development Center for "Magic Words" from *Songs and Stories of the Netsilik Eskimos*, translated by Edward Field from text collected by Knud Rasmussen.

Gray's Publishing Company Ltd., Sidney, British Columbia, for excerpt from *There Is My People Sleeping* by Sarain Stump. Copyright © 1970 by Sarain Stump. Excerpts from *Potlatch* by George Clutesi. Copyright © 1969.

Harper & Row Publishers, Inc., for excerpt from "Snow Country Weavers" by James Welch, from *Riding the Earthboy* 40, copyright © 1971. "Music" by Duane Niatum from *Digging out the Roots*, copyright © 1977 by Duane Niatum.

Harper & Row Publishers, Inc., and Simon Ortiz for poetry segments from *Going for the Rain*. Copyright © 1976 by Simon Ortiz.

Richard Hill for excerpt from "Native American Symbolism" from *Turtle*, Native American Center for the Living Arts quarterly, Summer 1979.

Roberta Hill for excerpt from "Song for Facing Winter" and for the poem "A Wish for Waving Goodbye." Copyright © 1978 by Roberta Hill. From *Sun Tracks* literary magazine, University of Arizona, Spring 1978.

Simon Ortiz for excerpts from "Song, Poetry, and Language: Expression and Perception," from *North American Indian Music and Dance*, Navajo Community College Press, copyright © 1977.

Wendy Rose for excerpt from "How I Came to Be a Graduate Student." Copyright © 1977 by Wendy Rose. For "Unstoppable" from *Contact 11 Journal, Academic Squaw*, Blue Cloud Press, Marvin, South Dakota, copyright © 1977 by Wendy Rose and from

# Notes

1. Gerald Vizenor, "Tribal People and the Poetic Image," *American Indian Art: Form and Tradition* (New York: E. P. Dutton, 1972), p. 18.
2. Bernard Katexac in a letter to the author from Nome, Alaska, June 1, 1979.
3. Edmund Carpenter, *Eskimo Realities* (New York: Holt, Rinehart & Winston, 1973) p. 75.
4. From an interview with Sarah Annanowt at Baker Lake, Northwest Territories, December 1978.
5. From Knud Rasmussen, cited in Charles Hofman, *Drum Dance* (Scarborough, Ontario: Gage Publishers, 1974), p. 20.
6. Dorothy Eber, *Pitseolak: Pictures Out of My Life* (Seattle: University of Washington Press, 1972).
7. Erna Siebert, *North American Indian Art* (London: Paul Hamlyn, 1967), pp. 26–27.
8. Edward S. Curtis, *The North American Indian* (New York: Johnson Reprint Co., 1970), 10:304.
9. Ibid., p. 324.
10. From an interview with the author, August 23, 1979.
11. From Franz Boas, *Ethnology of the Kwakiutl*, 35th Annual Report, Bureau of American Ethnology (Washington, D.C., 1921), p. 1310.
12. From an interview with the author, August 15, 1979.
13. From Knud Rasmussen, cited in Charles Hofman, *Drum Dance*, p. 40.
14. John Anson Warner, "Contemporary Algonkian Legend Painting," *American Indian Art Magazine*, Summer 1978, p. 60.
15. From an interview with the author, June 9, 1978.
16. From an interview with the author, October 9, 1979.
17. Richard Hill, "Native American Symbolism," *Native American Center for the Living Arts Quarterly*, Summer 1979.
18. From an interview with the author, October 11, 1979.
19. From interviews with the author, August 2 and September 7, 1979.
20. *South Dakota Review*, Summer 1969, p. 75.
21. John G. Neihardt, *Black Elk Speaks* (Lincoln: University of Nebraska Press, 1961), p. 4.
22. From interviews with the author, May 24 and 31, 1979.
23. Dorothy Dunn, *American Indian Painting of the Southwest and Plains Areas* (Albuquerque: University of New Mexico Press, 1969), p. 30.
24. Ibid., p. 208.
25. Fritz Scholder, in a letter to the author, August 13, 1979.
26. From an interview with Sarah Booth Conroy, *Washington Post*, May 6, 1978.
27. Herbert Joseph Spinden, trans., *Songs of the Tewa* (New York: Exposition of Indian Tribal Arts, 1933), p. 72.
28. Anthony Berlant and Mary Hunt Kahlenberg, *Walk in Beauty: The Navajo and Their Blankets* (New York: New York Graphic Society, 1977), pp. 3, 5.
29. From an interview with the author, July 31, 1978.
30. Simon Ortiz, *Going for the Rain* (New York: Harper & Row, 1976), p. 21.
31. Now the Wheelwright Museum of the American Indian.

32. From an interview with the author, May 8–9, 1978.

33. Washington Matthews, trans., *The Night Chant* (New York: Memoirs of the American Museum of Natural History, 1902), vol. 6, pp. 143–44.

34. J. J. Brody, *Indian Painters and White Patrons* (Albuquerque: University of New Mexico Press, 1971), p. 203.

35. From an interview with the author, July 27, 1978.

36. S. M. Barrett, ed., *Geronimo: His Own Story* (New York: Ballantine Books, by arrangement with E. P. Dutton, 1971), p. 29.

37. From an interview with the author, July 24, 1978.

38. From an interview with the author, July 26, 1978.

39. From an interview with the author, July 25, 1978.

40. Washington Matthews, trans., *The Mountain Chant*, 5th Annual Report, Bureau of American Ethnology (Washington, D.C., 1887), pp. 379–467.

41. George Clutesi, *Potlach* (Sidney, B.C.: Gray's Publishing Company, 1969), pp. 175–77.

42. Frank Waters, *Masked Gods* (New York: Ballantine Books, 1950), pp. 295–96.

43. Jerome Rothenberg, *Shaking the Pumpkin* (New York: Doubleday, 1972), p. 405.

44. "Indians in Hollywood," by Peggy Berry Hill, produced for *Horizons* by National Public Radio.

45. *Minneapolis Tribune*, April 24, 1978.

46. From an interview with the author, November 27, 1978.

47. Orpingalik, shaman and poet of the Netsilik Eskimo, in Knud Rasmussen, *The Netsilik Eskimos* (Copenhagen: Report of the 5th Thule Expedition, 1931), p. 321.

48. From an interview with the author, August 1, 1978.

49. From an interview with the author, August 24, 1979.

50. From a Modoc tale in Ella Clark, *Indian Legends of the Pacific Northwest* (Berkeley: University of California Press, 1953), p. 9.

51. From an interview with the author, July 28, 1978.

52. "Magic Words," from *Songs and Stories of the Netsilik Eskimos*. Translated by Edward Field, from text collected by Knud Rasmussen. Courtesy Education Development Center, Newton, Mass.

53. Wendy Rose, "How I Came to Be a Graduate Student," in *I Am the Fire of Time: The Voices of Native American Women*, ed. Jane B. Katz (New York: E. P. Dutton, 1977).

54. Frances Densmore, *American Indians and Their Music* (New York: The Women's Press, 1926), p. 71.

55. Duane Niatum, *Digging Out the Roots* (New York: Harper & Row, 1977), autobiographical notes.

56. Ibid., p. 46.

57. Leo W. Simmons, ed., *Sun Chief: The Autobiography of a Hopi Indian* (New Haven: Yale University Press, 1942), p. 99.

58. Alice Fletcher and Francis La Flesche, *The Omaha Tribe*, 27th Annual Report, Bureau of Ethnology (Washington, D.C., 1905–1906), pp. 571–73.

59. Ruth Underhill, *Autobiography of a Papago Woman*, American Anthropological Association Memoirs, Bulletin No. 46 (Washington, D.C., 1936), pp. 22–23.

60. From Rasmussen, cited in Charles Hofman, *Drum Dance*, p. 28.

61. Ruth Underhill, *Singing for Power* (Berkeley: University of California Press, 1977).

62. Margot Astrov, *American Indian Prose and Poetry* (New York: Capricorn Books, 1962), pp. 21–22.

63. Matthews, *The Night Chant*, Vol. 6, pp. 279–82.

64. Vizenor, "Tribal People and the Poetic Image," p. 19.

65. Sarain Stump, *There Is My People Sleeping* (Sidney, B.C.: Gray's Publishing, 1970).
66. Roberta Hill, "Song for Facing Winter," *Sun Tracks*, Spring 1978.
67. Vizenor, "Tribal People and the Poetic Image," p. 19.
68. *San Francisco Review of Books*, February 1979.
69. Prose segments by Gerald Vizenor, in *Growing Up in Minnesota: Ten Writers Remember Their Childhoods*, ed. Chester G. Anderson (Minneapolis: University of Minnesota Press, 1976).
70. From an interview with the author, August 3, 1979, in Minneapolis.
71. From an interview with the author, June 26, 1978.
72. Simon J. Ortiz, "Song, Poetry and Language: Expression and Perception," *North American Indian Music and Dance* (Navajo Community College, Tsaile, Arizona, 1977).
73. From autobiographical notes in *The Man to Send Rain Clouds*, ed. Kenneth Rosen (New York: Vintage Books, 1975).
74. Poetry segments by Simon J. Ortiz, *Going for the Rain* (New York: Harper & Row, 1976).
75. Ortiz, "Song, Poetry and Language."
76. From an interview with the author, July 31, 1978.
77. Leslie Silko, *Laguna Woman* (Greenfield Center, N.Y.: Greenfield Review Press, 1974).
78. Jack Davis, *Western American Literature*, November 1977, p. 243.
79. Adapted from material by Leslie Silko, *Laguna Woman* (Greenfield Center, N.Y.: Greenfield Review Press, 1974), and by Larry Evers and Denny Carr, "A Conversation with Leslie Marmon Silko," *Sun Tracks*, Fall 1976. Poetry segments from *Laguna Woman*.
80. From A. L. Kroeber, *Handbook of the Indians of California* (Washington, D.C.: Bureau of American Ethnology, 1925), p. 511.
81. N. Scott Momaday, *The Way to Rainy Mountain* (Albuquerque: University of New Mexico Press, 1969), p. 23.
82. N. Scott Momaday, *House Made of Dawn* (New York: Harper & Row, 1968), p. 25.
83. *Indian Voices* (San Francisco: The Indian Historian Press, 1970), p. 55.
84. From Momaday, *The Way to Rainy Mountain*, pp. 5–12.